The Self-H Book Fu. ....

Understand Your Fears & Overcome Them

By Donald F. Edgar

By reading this document, the reader agrees that under no circumstances is the author responsible for any losses, direct or indirect, which are incurred as a result of the use of the information contained within this document, including, but not limited to, — errors, omissions, or inaccuracies.

Content

Introduction

It can be tough being a man in today's world. For some men, the pressure of day-to-day life can build up and cause stress and anxiety that they may not know how to handle on their own. As a man myself, I understand both the physical and mental struggles faced by those living with these difficult emotions – which is why I wrote this book. This book is designed to provide practical tips, techniques, and strategies for overcoming anxiety so you can lead a healthier and happier life. So if you're looking for advice on managing your emotions effectively or curious about some of the best ways to tackle worry, fear and panic attacks, then keep reading - this guide could be just what you need!

It all started when I got into a relationship. Everything had been going great up until that point, but the minute we both decided to get serious, I started feeling anxious and overwhelmed. At first, I thought it was just normal jitters – after all, relationships are never easy! But as time passed, my worries deepened, and soon enough, they took over my life.

I tried to ignore it at first by pretending everything was okay but eventually realized there was no way around it; I needed help. So with a heavy heart and trembling hands, I booked an appointment with a therapist who could help me understand why this sudden anxiety had taken hold of me.

At first, the therapy sessions were daunting because talking about my feelings is not something that comes naturally to me. But gradually, things did start to change - as if someone had flicked on the light switch in my mind - as newfound clarity began to take shape within me from week-to-week discussions with my therapist about how best to manage these thoughts and feelings towards myself and others in healthy ways.

As months passed, our sessions became more like conversations rather than therapeutic analyses, making it so much easier for me to open up about whatever came across my mind during each session. Over time the intensity of these anxieties lessened considerably until one day, they simply vanished altogether! And while it took some getting used to (after all, this journey wasn't always easy), ultimately seeking out professional help turned out to be one of the best decisions of my life!

1. Understanding Anxiety

1.1.   Understanding the symptoms of anxiety

Anxiety is like a storm cloud that follows you around, casting a shadow over your thoughts and actions. It can make you feel uneasy, nervous, and on edge, as if you're constantly waiting for something bad to happen. It can be a difficult and overwhelming feeling to cope with, but with the right tools and support, it can be managed and eventually dissipated.

- Anxiety is normal, and everyone experiences it at some point in their life
- There are different types of anxiety, each with unique symptoms

- Anxiety can be caused by several factors, including stress, genetics, and the environment
- Some common symptoms of anxiety include feeling overwhelmed or out of control, racing thoughts, excessive worry, and physical symptoms such as headaches and nausea

As a hurt man, you may be familiar with how anxiety can take over your life. Anxiety can interfere with relationships and make everyday tasks difficult to accomplish. But what is anxiety exactly? Feel supported in knowing that even small changes over time can make a big difference in reducing the effects of anxiety.

As a man, it can be easy to overlook anxiety symptoms. Anxiety can look and feel different for everyone, and men in particular. This can lead to some confusion when it comes to understanding these symptoms. Men must familiarize themselves with how anxiety feels to be able to recognize and manage it. Common signs of anxiety may include difficulty concentrating, heart palpitations or shortness of breath, restlessness or feeling on edge, muscle tension, trouble sleeping, irritability or anger outbursts, and increased worry or anxious thoughts and feelings if you notice any combination of these signs. With proper understanding, you can better address your anxiety for improved well-being.

Common types of anxiety disorders and their symptoms :

1. Generalized anxiety disorder
2. Social anxiety disorder
3. Panic disorder
4. Obsessive-compulsive disorder
5. Posttraumatic stress disorder
6. Phobias

1.1.1. Generalized anxiety disorder (GAD)

Anxiety is something everyone experiences in their life, but those suffering from generalized anxiety disorder (GAD) feel it at a constant and more significant level. GAD emerges when individuals feel excessive worry and tension on an almost daily basis. They can have difficulty controlling these worries, which can cause physical symptoms like restlessness, shortness of breath, and even headaches. Mental congestion arises from an individual's inability to relax or clear their mind from stressful thoughts. It's essential to take steps to manage anxiety and seek help if needed so that it doesn't become too overwhelming or disruptive in everyday life; talking with a therapist or doctor can be insightful and helpful in managing anxiety.

Gavin had grown up feeling like something was wrong with him, but he never quite knew what it was. He'd been told by his parents that he was too sensitive for his good and that he needed to toughen up. But no matter how hard he tried, Gavin couldn't seem to shake the feelings of unease and anxiety that seemed to follow him everywhere.

When Gavin got older, things only got worse. Simple tasks began to feel overwhelming; walking into a room full of people or even having a conversation felt like an insurmountable challenge at times. He became increasingly isolated as fear took over every aspect of his life until eventually, all Gavin could do was stay in bed and dread the day ahead.

It wasn't until after years of this struggle -- well into adulthood -- that Gavin finally decided to visit a specialist to get some help for his condition. After doing extensive research on anxiety disorder treatments, Gavin found out what many others already knew: there is no cure-all solution when it comes to managing mental health issues like generalized anxiety disorder (GAD). Instead, it requires careful management through medication, therapy sessions and lifestyle changes such as exercise and diet adjustments.

Although these steps helped alleviate some aspects of GAD for Gavin over time, there were still moments where the old familiar feelings would return stronger than ever before - especially during stressful periods or transitions in life, such as starting college or moving away from home for work purposes. Even so, armed with newfound knowledge about himself thanks to visiting specialists late in life combined with coping mechanisms developed through practice and experience - these moments didn't last long anymore compared to before when they used to overwhelm him completely without warning..

No one can truly understand what living with GAD feels like without experiencing its effects firsthand – yet despite everything he has gone through because of it – somehow Gavin still manages to find beauty amidst all this chaos within everyday life. That's why no matter how difficult things get sometimes,he takes solace in knowing nothing can take away from joys derived from small moments shared between friends, loved ones,and strangers alike, which helps make each passing day just a little bit easier .

1.1.2. Social anxiety disorder

Social ****anxiety disorder is a condition in which an individual experiences intense fear and avoidance of social situations. This can manifest in a range of physical and psychological symptoms, such as rapid heart rate, difficulty speaking, excessive sweating, trembling, and nausea. People who struggle with this condition often experience feelings of low self-worth, shame, or embarrassment because they feel they cannot control their reactions to the environment around them. It is important to understand that social anxiety disorder is a complex problem that affects millions of people around the world. With treatment and understanding, it can be managed - those who are affected deserve compassionate care and support in finding strategies for coping with social situations that may feel overwhelming at first.

He was a young man who had lived his entire youth suffering from social anxiety disorder. Growing up, he felt like he didn't belong anywhere - the crippling fear of judgment and embarrassment prevented him from forming meaningful relationships with other people. He kept to himself, avoiding all possible contact with strangers or anyone outside his family circle.

His days were spent in solitude – alone at home or in school, surrounded by unfamiliar faces that seemed to be judging him no matter what he did. All of these feelings and sensations compounded until one day, it became too much for him to bear any longer, tears streaming down his face as he realized how isolated and lonely he truly was.

But over time, something changed inside of him - an inner strength slowly began to take hold as he learned how to manage his anxiety-ridden thoughts and emotions through formal therapy sessions as well as self-reflection and meditation techniques. He slowly started making progress towards accepting himself for whom he is rather than worrying about what others thought of him - an important step in overcoming the struggles associated with living with social anxiety disorder.

It took years before this young man finally reached a point where being around other people wasn't completely paralyzing anymore; although there are still moments when overwhelming fear takes control, they are becoming fewer and farther between each passing day. It has been a long journey filled with many difficult challenges along the way, but now that same young man stands tall on solid ground once again, knowing that anything is possible if you have courage enough within your heart!He was a young man who had lived his entire youth suffering from a social anxiety disorder. Growing up, he felt like he didn't belong anywhere - the crippling fear of judgment and embarrassment prevented him from forming meaningful relationships with other people. He kept to himself, avoiding all possible contact with strangers or anyone outside his family circle.

His days were spent in solitude – alone at home or in school, surrounded by unfamiliar faces that seemed to be judging him no matter what he did. All of these feelings and sensations compounded until one day, it became too much for him to bear any longer; tears streaming down his face as he realized how isolated and lonely he truly was.

But over time, something changed inside of him - an inner strength slowly began to take hold as he learned how to manage his anxiety-ridden thoughts and emotions through formal therapy sessions as well as self-reflection and meditation techniques. He slowly started making progress towards accepting himself for whom he is rather than worrying about what others thought of him - an important step in overcoming the struggles associated with living with social anxiety disorder.

It took years before this young man finally reached a point where being around other people wasn't completely paralyzing anymore; although there are still moments when overwhelming fear takes control, they are becoming fewer and farther with each passing day. It has been a long journey filled with many difficult challenges along the way but now that same young man stands tall on solid ground once again, knowing that anything is possible if you have courage enough within your heart!

1.1.3. Panic disorder

Panic disorder is a serious mental health concern faced by many, characterized by sudden and overwhelming feelings of fear, worry, and uncertainty. Often accompanied by physical symptoms like chest pain, nausea, shortness of breath, and trembling, panic disorder can be disabling and difficult to cope with. While the exact cause of the panic disorder is not fully understood, research suggests that a combination of biological, psychological, and environmental factors may play a role in its development. Treatment for panic disorder includes evidence-based approaches such as cognitive-behavioral therapy (CBT), which encourages individuals to challenge the negative thoughts associated with attacks and confront their fears so they can eventually live without debilitating symptoms of anxiety. Recovery from panic disorder is possible.

Growing up was never easy for Jack. From a young age, anxiety and panic had taken hold of his life; it seemed as if every day he stepped outside his door there was something new to be afraid of. He would experience bouts of intense fear, often so severe that he felt like the world around him was closing in on him.

It wasn't until Jack reached high school that he finally realized what was happening—that these feelings were symptoms of an extreme panic disorder. While this realization didn't make things any easier, it did provide a sense of relief; at least now Jack knew why everything felt so scary all the time.

But with knowledge came responsibility: managing and controlling his own emotions became more important than ever before. It required immense amounts of discipline and self-control, especially during times when the thoughts in his head began to spiral out of control. Even simple tasks like walking down the hallway or attending class could become overwhelming very quickly.

And yet, despite all this difficulty, Jack's strength shone through—he refused to give into despair or let himself be defined by his condition alone. Instead, he worked hard every day to keep pushing forward no matter what obstacles lay ahead; even when faced with uncertainty and fear about how things would turn out tomorrow or next week or months from now, somehow he managed to persist against all odds—to keep going one step at a time until eventually reaching the place where we find him today: contented but still cautious nonetheless about whatever else lies ahead on life's winding journey for him...

1.1.4. Obsessive-compulsive disorder (OCD)

Obsessive-compulsive disorder (OCD) is an often-debilitating mental illness that affects many people. It can manifest itself in a variety of ways, such as with intrusive thoughts, an excessive need for certain routines or rituals, or even physical tics. It is important to understand that those with OCD cannot simply 'shake it off.' There is no universal treatment for OCD, but various forms of therapy combined with medication have been shown to help lessen the symptoms and make daily life more manageable. If you are struggling with OCD, know that you are not alone and seek help from a medical professional so you can live your life to its fullest potential.

As a young man, I had always felt like an outsider. People around me seemed to be able to effortlessly go through their lives while my mind was consumed by intrusive thoughts and constant worries. My obsessive-compulsive disorder (OCD) made it difficult for me to engage in social activities, maintain relationships, and even keep up with my studies. Every day I would obsess over things that were out of my control; the smallest thing could send my mind into a tailspin of anxiety and panic.

I tried hard to make sense of it all - why did I feel this way? Why couldn't I just relax? To try to manage it, I developed rigid rules for myself: doing certain tasks in a specific order or repeating actions multiple times until they felt "right." But no matter how hard I tried, these rituals didn't seem to help much - if anything, they only increased the intensity of my OCD symptoms.

I was ashamed of this condition because people didn't understand what was going on inside me; even those close to me looked at me with confusion when they saw me engaged in some strange behavior due to the OCD impulses controlling my body. It wasn't until years later that more awareness about mental health issues began circulating that allowed people like myself some relief from stigma and judgmental looks.

My life is still not easy but now, at least, there's understanding and acceptance among family members and friends who know how hard living with OCD can be at times. Through therapy sessions, medication adjustments, and lifestyle changes such as learning relaxation techniques – which are incredibly helpful – as well as joining support groups where one can learn more about managing the condition better, have helped immensely along the journey towards recovery from this debilitating illness.

1.1.5. Posttraumatic stress disorder

Posttraumatic stress disorder, or PTSD, is a very real and difficult reality for those who have experienced trauma. It can manifest itself in many ways such as flashbacks, nightmares, mood swings, and feelings of isolation and shame. People who go through trauma often experience changes in their lives, including diminished academic performance or job loss. These individuals need to be shown compassion and understanding. With proper treatment that includes therapy and medication, individuals with PTSD stand the best chance of moving forward with strength and resilience. It is important that we recognize this condition so that those suffering from it can receive the support they need to ultimately heal.

Adam had lived his whole life with complex post-traumatic stress disorder. It had been a long, hard journey for him to get to this point in his life where he was finally starting to feel somewhat normal again. But even now, after so many years of therapy and medications, there were still moments of intense anxiety that seemed impossible to escape.

He remembered back when he was just a young boy, running around the playground with all the other kids like nothing was wrong. Then one day he heard loud screams coming from inside his house - it was his dad beating up his mom, and before Adam knew it, everything changed forever. He felt so helpless as he watched them fight and eventually saw his father dragged away by the police - never to be seen again.

It felt like only yesterday that Adam had been filled with fear every time someone raised their voice or slammed a door shut too loudly; an invisible hand would grip at him tightly and wouldn't let go until somebody hugged him tightly enough that they could take some of the pain away from what he'd gone through as a child. His heart would race faster than ever when something unexpected happened, no matter how small or insignificant it seemed on the outside - but for Adam, those little things were terrifying reminders of what once happened in that same house so long ago…

These days though, after many years working through counseling sessions and taking medication specifically designed for PTSD sufferers like himself; although there are still times when memories come flooding back alongside feelings of dread - these days Adam is more able to manage them better because now, he has strategies which can help calm himself down whenever any kind of trigger comes along unexpectedly into view or sound form...

It's taken lots of practice, but over time, Adam has learned how best deal with these kinds of episodes, whether its deep breathing techniques or simply talking out loud about what's happening internally – each method gives him comfort knowing regardless if today is better than yesterday – tomorrow will always bring hope!

Explanation of the book's goal and what readers can expect to learn

This self-help anxiety book for men provides readers with comprehensive techniques, educational opportunities, and psychological strategies to manage current and future levels of stress and anxiety. Readers can expect to gain deep insight into the causes of their anxiety, as well as develop useful coping mechanisms and empowerment skills that will help them live a healthier, more balanced lifestyle. Furthermore, it provides an in-depth understanding of the relationship between anxiety and social behaviour, the biology of an anxious brain, and more. This type of book helps readers recognize how times of change and uncertainty can impact mental health and how to maintain individual progress over time. You will learn about key values for creating an environment conducive to personal growth, finding support from others in similar situations, and engaging in meaningful activities that support goals related to well-being both short-term and long-term.

1.2.   Understanding the causes of anxiety

Biological causes: Research suggests that anxiety may be caused by an imbalance of chemicals in the brain, such as serotonin and dopamine. Additionally, certain genetic predispositions and physical conditions, such as thyroid dysfunction, may also contribute to the development of anxiety in men.

Anxiety is a common mental health condition that affects people of all ages and genders. However, research has shown that men and women may experience anxiety differently, with men being less likely to seek help for their symptoms. One possible explanation for these differences is the role of biology in shaping men's susceptibility to anxiety. Here I will explore how biology can affect anxiety in men, with a focus on the effects of hormones and genetics.

One way that biology can affect anxiety in men is through the action of hormones. Testosterone, the primary male sex hormone, plays a critical role in regulating mood and behavior. Research has shown that low levels of testosterone are associated with an increased risk of anxiety, while higher levels may help to reduce anxiety symptoms. For example, men with low levels of testosterone have been found to have lower levels of GABA, a neurotransmitter that plays a key role in regulating anxiety. Furthermore, studies have shown that testosterone replacement therapy can help to reduce anxiety symptoms in men with low levels of the hormone.

Another way that biology can affect anxiety in men is through genetics. Studies have found that genetic factors account for a significant portion of the risk for anxiety disorders. In particular, genetic variants in genes that regulate the activity of neurotransmitters and other molecules that are involved in the brain's stress response have been linked to an increased risk of anxiety. Additionally, a family history of anxiety is also a risk factor for anxiety disorder. This suggests that men who have a family history of anxiety may be more susceptible to developing the disorder due to inherited genetic factors.

Additionally, studies also indicate that brain structure also plays a role in anxiety disorder among men. Men with an enlarged Amygdala, a region of the brain involved in emotional processing and stress, were found to have a greater risk of developing an anxiety disorder. And also, studies of brain activity have shown that people with anxiety disorders tend to have overactive amygdala and underactive prefrontal cortex, leading to a heightened state of stress and anxiety.

In conclusion, biology plays a significant role in shaping men's susceptibility to anxiety. Hormones such as testosterone and genetics can both contribute to the development of anxiety disorders in men. Understanding the biological underpinnings of anxiety in men can help to improve diagnosis and treatment for this condition and provide men with the support and resources they need to manage their symptoms effectively.

Environmental causes: Exposure to traumatic events, such as physical or emotional abuse, may lead to the development of anxiety in men. Furthermore, stressful life events, such as the loss of a loved one or job, can also contribute to anxiety.

The environment in which a person lives can have a significant impact on their mental health, including their levels of anxiety. For men specifically, the environment can play a crucial role in shaping their experiences of anxiety and how they cope with it.

One way in which the environment can affect anxiety in men is through the presence of stressors. Stressors are external factors that can cause an individual to feel overwhelmed and anxious. These can include things like financial difficulties, relationship problems, or job insecurity. Men who are exposed to chronic stressors, such as those living in poverty or in dangerous neighborhoods, may be more likely to experience anxiety than those who are not.

Another way in which the environment can affect anxiety in men is through social norms and expectations. Society often expects men to be strong and emotionally stoic, which can make it difficult for men to express their feelings or ask for help when they are struggling with anxiety. This can lead to men feeling isolated and unable to cope with their symptoms, resulting in an exacerbation of their anxiety.

Additionally, the physical environment can also play a role in anxiety, For example, the air and noise pollution in an urban environment can be a source of stress and anxiety, and the feeling of safety and a sense of belonging in the community, or lack of it can also significantly affect mental wellbeing.

Furthermore, the environment can also affect anxiety through a lack of access to mental health resources. Men who live in rural areas, for example, may have limited access to mental health care and may be less likely to seek help for their anxiety. Similarly, men who are uninsured or underinsured may find it difficult to afford mental health treatment, which can lead to their anxiety going untreated.

In conclusion, the environment can affect anxiety in men in a variety of ways, including through the presence of stressors, societal expectations and norms, the physical environment, and lack of access to mental health resources. It is important for individuals, communities, and society as a whole to recognize and address these environmental factors in order to support men in managing and reducing their anxiety.

It is important to note that research about this topic is ongoing and findings may vary based on cultures and countries, as well as based on different groups of men, as experiences and backgrounds can vary greatly.

Psychological causes: Men may develop anxiety as a result of negative thinking patterns, such as excessive worry or rumination. Additionally, perfectionism, and a tendency to avoid or suppress emotions, may also contribute to the development of anxiety.

Write me an essay on developing anxiety as a result of negative thinking patterns, such as excessive worry or rumination. Additionally, perfectionism and a tendency to avoid or suppress emotions. Anxiety is a common psychological disorder that affects a significant portion of the population. It is characterized by excessive worry and fears about various aspects of life. Many different factors can contribute to the development of anxiety, but one of the most significant is negative thinking patterns.

This includes excessive worry, rumination, perfectionism, and a tendency to avoid or suppress emotions. Excessive worry is a common feature of anxiety disorders, and it is characterized by an excessive and unrealistic fear of future events. People who excessively worry tend to focus on negative outcomes and overestimate the likelihood of negative events occurring. This can cause them to feel constantly on edge and can make it difficult for them to relax or enjoy activities. Rumination is another type of negative thinking that is closely related to excessive worry. It involves dwelling on negative thoughts or emotions, and it can make it difficult for people to let go of past experiences and move forward. People who ruminate tend to feel stuck in their thoughts, and they can become preoccupied with past mistakes or regrets. Perfectionism is another contributing factor to the development of anxiety. People who are perfectionists tend to set impossibly high standards for themselves and others, and they are often critical of themselves and others. This can lead to feelings of inadequacy and self-doubt, which can trigger anxiety symptoms. Lastly, a tendency to avoid or suppress emotions is also linked to anxiety. People who avoid or suppress their emotions tend to bottle them up and suppress them, rather than deal with them in a healthy way. This can lead to unresolved emotions and unresolved issues, which can contribute to the development of anxiety over time. Overall, developing anxiety as a result of negative thinking patterns is a complex process. These patterns, such as excessive worry, rumination, perfectionism, and a tendency to avoid or suppress emotions, can contribute to the development of anxiety over time. However, with proper treatment and therapy, these negative thinking patterns can be identified and changed, and individuals can learn to manage their anxiety symptoms more effectively. It is important to seek help as soon as possible when experiencing symptoms of anxiety and to seek professional help to understand the root causes of one's symptoms. A therapist or counselor can teach you skills and strategies for changing negative thinking patterns, learning to manage emotions, and reducing anxiety. They can also teach you how to identify triggers and high-risk situations and develop coping strategies for when anxiety does occur. with the right help and support, individuals can learn to manage their anxiety symptoms, overcome negative thinking patterns and live a more fulfilling life.

Socio-Cultural causes: societal expectations and stereotypes for men to always appear "strong" and in control can put undue pressure on men and may contribute to anxiety. Similarly, the reluctance of men to seek help or express their emotions may lead to the development or prolongation of anxiety.

Society often holds certain expectations and stereotypes for men, one of which is that they should always appear "strong" and in control. This expectation can put undue pressure on men and contribute to the development of anxiety. When men feel the need to constantly project a strong and in-control image, they may feel as though they cannot show any signs of vulnerability or weakness. This can lead to feelings of isolation and disconnection, as men may feel that they cannot be their true selves in front of others. Additionally, men may feel the pressure to always have the answers and to never admit to not knowing something, which can lead to increased stress and anxiety.

Another issue is that of the feminist anti-men movement, which has emerged in recent years. While the intentions behind this movement are to empower women and to address the patriarchal systems in place, it has also led to a shift in the way that men are perceived and treated in society. Men may feel as though they are being blamed for the struggles of women, and that they are no longer valued or respected in the same way that they once were. This can lead to feelings of shame, resentment, and anxiety.

However, it's important to note that being open about your feelings is becoming more accepted and normalized as society is changing; it is becoming the new "cool" in the sense of expressing yourself. It is essential to note that both men and women are affected by societal expectations and stereotypes, but men may feel particularly vulnerable when it comes to seeking help and expressing their emotions. Therefore, breaking the stereotype of the strong, silent man is an important step towards creating a more balanced and healthy society.

In conclusion, societal expectations and stereotypes for men to always appear "strong" and in control can put undue pressure on men and contribute to the development of anxiety. The feminist anti-men movement may also have an effect on men's drive to achieve things and their self-esteem. Furthermore, being open about one's feelings is becoming more accepted and normalized in society, which is a positive change. It is important for society to recognize and challenge these harmful stereotypes, to reduce the pressure on men, and to create a culture where men can feel comfortable seeking help and expressing their emotions without fear of judgment.

Substance Abuse: Men who abuse substances such as alcohol or drugs may develop anxiety as a result of their substance use. Additionally, certain medications, such as antidepressants, may cause anxiety as a side effect.

Substance abuse and anxiety are closely related, and men are more likely to abuse substances, such as alcohol and drugs, and develop anxiety as a result. Substance abuse can lead to a number of negative consequences, including anxiety, and can become a vicious cycle, as anxiety can lead to further substance abuse. Additionally, social isolation is one of the reasons that men may turn to substance abuse as a means of coping with their feelings.

One of the ways in which substance abuse can lead to anxiety is through the development of a substance use disorder. When a person becomes dependent on a substance, they may experience withdrawal symptoms when they try to stop using it. These symptoms can include anxiety, as well as other physical and psychological symptoms, which can make it difficult for an individual to quit using the substance. Additionally, continued use of the substance can lead to tolerance and increase the dose needed, which in turn can lead to greater anxiety as the body becomes reliant on the substance.

Another way in which substance abuse can lead to anxiety is through the direct effects of the substance on the brain. Certain drugs and alcohol can alter the chemical balance of the brain, leading to changes in mood, including increased anxiety. Additionally, some substances, such as stimulants, can cause feelings of agitation and nervousness, which can mimic symptoms of anxiety.

Social isolation can be a significant contributing factor to substance abuse in men. Men may turn to substances as a way to cope with feelings of isolation and disconnection. This can lead to the development of substance use disorders, which can further contribute to feelings of isolation and disconnection, creating a vicious cycle.

It's also important to note that certain medications, such as antidepressants, may cause anxiety as a side effect. This is because these medications affect the levels of certain chemicals in the brain and may result in anxiety as a side effect. This is not always the case but it's important to consult with a doctor if such symptoms appear.

In conclusion, substance abuse and consequential anxiety in men is a serious issue that can have a significant impact on mental health. Men may turn to substances as a way to cope with feelings of isolation and disconnection, which can lead to the development of substance use disorders, which can further contribute to feelings of isolation and disconnection. Additionally, certain medications, such as antidepressants, may cause anxiety as a side effect.

Medical Condition: Chronic Medical conditions such as asthma, diabetes, heart disease, etc, can contribute to anxiety.

Chronic medical conditions, such as asthma, diabetes, and heart disease, can have a significant impact on an individual's mental health, including the development of anxiety. These conditions can be a source of stress and uncertainty, leading to feelings of worry, fear, and helplessness. Additionally, the physical symptoms of these conditions can exacerbate anxiety and make it difficult for individuals to manage their symptoms.

Asthma, for example, can cause individuals to feel short of breath, chest tightness, and coughing, which can be frightening and trigger feelings of panic and anxiety. Similarly, diabetes can cause individuals to experience fatigue, frequent urination, and changes in blood sugar levels, which can lead to feelings of anxiety and uncertainty. Heart disease, on the other hand, can cause chest pain, shortness of breath, and other symptoms that can be alarming and contribute to anxiety.

Furthermore, individuals with chronic medical conditions may also experience social isolation and difficulty in their daily activities, which in turn can contribute to feelings of anxiety. They may feel limited in their ability to participate in their favorite activities, and may feel like they are missing out on life experiences. This can lead to feelings of hopelessness, depression, and anxiety.

Additionally, Chronic Medical conditions can lead to financial stress, as they often require expensive and ongoing treatment. This can cause feelings of worry and stress, which can contribute to the development of anxiety.

Moreover, Chronic Medical conditions can also affect sleep patterns, and those with chronic medical conditions may find it difficult to get a good night's sleep, which can contribute to feelings of anxiety and irritability.

In conclusion, chronic medical conditions such as asthma, diabetes, and heart disease can have a significant impact on mental health, including the development of anxiety. These conditions can cause physical symptoms that can exacerbate anxiety and can lead to feelings of social isolation, financial stress, and difficulty in daily activities. It's important for individuals with chronic medical conditions to have access to mental health support, to help them manage their anxiety symptoms, and to improve their overall quality of life. Additionally, it's also important to manage chronic medical conditions with the help of a medical professional to avoid any complications or exacerbation of symptoms.

1.2.1. The role of neurotransmitters and hormones in anxiety

The role of neurotransmitters and hormones in anxiety is a complex and multi-faceted issue. The nervous system, hormones, and brain chemistry are all interconnected, and they all play a crucial role in the development and maintenance of anxiety.

Neurotransmitters are chemical messengers in the brain that transmit signals between nerve cells. Several neurotransmitters have been found to play a role in the development of anxiety, including serotonin, GABA, and dopamine.

GABA, serotonin, and dopamine are three neurotransmitters that have been found to play a significant role in the development and maintenance of anxiety in men. The proper functioning of these neurotransmitters is essential for regulating mood and emotions, and imbalances in these neurotransmitters can contribute to the development of anxiety.

GABA (Gamma-aminobutyric acid) is an inhibitory neurotransmitter that helps to calm down the nervous system. When GABA levels are low, the nervous system can become overactive, leading to feelings of anxiety, nervousness, and restlessness. Research has shown that individuals with anxiety disorders have lower levels of GABA than those without the condition. Low GABA levels have been linked to an increased activity of excitatory neurotransmitters such as glutamate, which can contribute to feelings of anxiety.

Serotonin is a neurotransmitter that is involved in regulating mood, anxiety, and various bodily functions such as sleep and appetite. Serotonin is known as the "feel-good" neurotransmitter, and low levels of serotonin have been linked to the development of anxiety disorders. Research suggests that low serotonin levels can lead to an overactive stress response, which can contribute to feelings of anxiety and worry. This can be associated with specific brain regions, as studies have shown that low serotonin levels in the hippocampus and amygdala, which are regions involved in emotion regulation, are linked to anxiety disorders.

Dopamine is another neurotransmitter that plays a role in regulating mood and anxiety. Dopamine is a neurotransmitter involved in the reward system and is essential for motivation, pleasure, and the ability to experience rewards. Low levels of dopamine have been linked to feelings of anxiety and depression, and it is thought that this may be due to its role in regulating the reward system in the brain. When dopamine levels are low, the reward system may not work as well, and this can lead to feelings of anxiety, hopelessness and despair.

Hormones also play a crucial role in the development of anxiety. Hormones such as cortisol and adrenaline are released in response to stress.

Adrenaline and cortisol are hormones that play a crucial role in the development and maintenance of anxiety in men. These hormones are released in response to stress and can contribute to the development of anxiety by increasing heart rate, blood pressure, and muscle tension.

Adrenaline, also known as epinephrine, is a hormone that is released by the adrenal glands in response to stress. It is known as the "fight or flight" hormone and is responsible for preparing the body for physical activity by increasing heart rate, blood pressure, and glucose levels in the bloodstream. When adrenaline is released, it can lead to physical symptoms such as increased heart rate, shaking, and sweating, which can be mistaken as symptoms of anxiety. These symptoms can be perceived as threatening and can lead to feelings of panic and anxiety.

Cortisol is another hormone that is released in response to stress. Cortisol is known as the "stress hormone" and is responsible for regulating the body's response to stress. It increases glucose levels in the bloodstream, suppresses the immune system, and increases heart rate, blood pressure, and muscle tension. Elevated cortisol levels can contribute to feelings of anxiety, nervousness, and restlessness. Chronic stress can lead to prolonged cortisol release, which in turn can lead to chronic anxiety.

It is important to note that adrenaline and cortisol play a crucial role in the body's stress response and are not necessarily bad. They are necessary for survival, allowing the body to react quickly to potential dangers. However, when these hormones are released excessively or for prolonged periods, they can contribute to the development of anxiety.

Additionally, hormones such as Thyroxine and Thyroid Stimulating Hormones can also play a role in the development of anxiety. Hormonal imbalances such as hypothyroidism can affect the levels of these hormones and in turn, can contribute to anxiety symptoms.

In conclusion, neurotransmitters and hormones play a crucial role in the development of anxiety in men. Several neurotransmitters, such as serotonin, GABA, and dopamine, have been found to be involved in the development of anxiety. Additionally, hormones such as cortisol, adrenaline, and thyroid hormones also contribute to the development of anxiety.

1.2.2. How past experiences can affect the development of anxiety

Exposure to traumatic events, such as physical or emotional abuse, can have a significant and long-lasting impact on an individual's mental health, including the development of anxiety. Trauma can be defined as any event or experience that causes significant psychological distress, and this can include physical or emotional abuse.

Physical abuse can include any form of physical violence, such as hitting, punching, or sexually assaulting. Exposure to physical abuse can lead to physical injury, as well as long-term psychological effects, such as anxiety. The physical symptoms of abuse, such as pain and injuries, can be traumatic in and of themselves and can also serve as constant reminders of the abuse. This can lead to feelings of fear, guilt, and shame and can contribute to the development of anxiety disorders.

Emotional abuse, such as verbal abuse, manipulation, and control, can be just as damaging as physical abuse. Emotional abuse can leave individuals feeling isolated, worthless, and powerless. These feelings can contribute to the development of anxiety disorders, as well as depression and post-traumatic stress disorder (PTSD).

Trauma can also lead to changes in brain chemistry, which can contribute to the development of anxiety. Research has shown that exposure to traumatic events can lead to changes in neurotransmitters, such as serotonin and GABA, which can contribute to the development of anxiety disorders. Additionally, traumatic events can lead to chronic stress, which can also contribute to changes in brain chemistry, leading to the development of anxiety.

Furthermore, life events such as the loss of a loved one or loss of a job can be extremely stressful and can contribute to the development of anxiety in men. The loss of a loved one, whether it be through death or separation, can be a traumatic experience that can leave a person feeling overwhelmed, sad, and alone. This can lead to feelings of anxiety as the individual struggles to come to terms with their loss and adjust to life without the person who has died or left.

Similarly, losing a job can also be a very stressful event that can lead to feelings of anxiety. Job loss can bring about financial insecurity, a loss of identity and self-worth, and uncertainty about the future. It can also be associated with social isolation and being seen as a failure by others. These feelings can lead to increased levels of stress and can contribute to the development of anxiety.

In conclusion, exposure to traumatic events, such as physical or emotional abuse, loss of a loved one, or job loss, can have a significant and long-lasting impact on an individual's mental health, including the development of anxiety. Trauma can lead to changes in brain chemistry, which can contribute to the development of anxiety disorders.

2. Mindfulness And Self-Awareness

2.1. An introduction to mindfulness and its benefits for reducing anxiety

Mindfulness is the practice of being present and engaged in the current moment without judgment. It involves paying attention to one's thoughts, feelings, and physical sensations in a non-reactive and non-judgmental way. This approach has been found to be effective in reducing anxiety. Regular practice of mindfulness has been shown to improve symptoms of anxiety disorders, including panic disorder, social anxiety disorder, and generalized anxiety disorder, as well as reduce symptoms of stress. Mindfulness practice can also help individuals to recognize the early warning signs of anxiety and respond to them in a more positive way. Furthermore, Mindfulness-Based Cognitive Therapy (MBCT) has been found to be an effective treatment for people who have recurrent depression. Through regular practice, individuals may be better able to manage their thoughts and emotions, and respond to stressful situations in a more adaptive way.

Jake had always been a shy and introverted person, but in recent years, his social anxiety had become debilitating. He found it difficult to interact with others, and even simple tasks like going to the grocery store or meeting new people felt impossible.

Jake's anxiety affected every aspect of his life. He struggled to maintain friendships and romantic relationships and found it hard to keep a job. He felt isolated and alone, and it seemed like there was no way out of his suffering.

One day, a friend suggested that Jake try meditation. He had heard that it could help with anxiety and was willing to try anything to improve his situation. So, Jake began a daily meditation practice.

At first, it was difficult for Jake to quiet his mind and focus on his breath. He found his thoughts constantly drifting to his worries and fears. But with time and practice, Jake began to notice small changes. He felt calmer and more centered throughout the day, and his mind felt less cluttered.

As Jake's meditation practice progressed, he began to gain a new perspective on his anxiety. He realized that his anxious thoughts were just thoughts, not facts and that he had the power to observe them without getting caught up in them. He learned to detach himself from the constant chatter in his mind, and it allowed him to be more present at the moment.

With the help of meditation, Jake's anxiety began to decrease, and he felt more confident in social situations. He started going out more, reconnecting with old friends and even found the courage to start dating again. He landed a new job, and he enjoyed it, and he found that he was able to interact with his colleagues and clients without feeling so nervous. He felt like a whole new person.

Thanks to his daily meditation practice, Jake was able to return to a healthy social life. He felt more connected to others, and his newfound inner peace allowed him to appreciate the beauty of life in a way that he never thought possible.

Meditation had changed everything for Jake, and it was a lifelong tool that he was going to use to keep himself on track he felt grateful for his friend who had suggested it to him. He knew that he would always have moments of anxiety, but with the help of meditation, he felt empowered to face them with grace and courage.

2.2. Techniques for becoming more self-aware, including journaling, meditation, and therapy

2.2.1. Journaling

Journaling is the act of writing down one's thoughts and feelings in a diary or journal. It can be done in any format, whether it be a physical notebook or a digital document. The act of writing has been shown to have therapeutic benefits for people dealing with anxiety. Studies have shown that journaling can reduce symptoms of anxiety by helping to process difficult emotions, identify patterns of thinking and behavior, and increase self-awareness.

When it comes to managing anxiety, journaling can be used in a number of ways. One approach is called "expressive writing," which involves writing about difficult or traumatic experiences in order to process them and gain a better understanding of one's emotions. By putting thoughts and feelings on paper, individuals can gain a sense of control over them and gain a deeper understanding of the root cause of their anxiety. This can help to reduce anxiety symptoms and promote emotional healing.

Another way to use journaling as a tool for managing anxiety is through "cognitive-behavioral journaling." This approach involves identifying and challenging negative thoughts and patterns of behavior that contribute to anxiety. Journaling allows individuals to record their thoughts and feelings at the moment and reflect on them later. By examining negative thought patterns and identifying the triggers that lead to them, individuals can learn to change the way they think about anxiety-provoking situations, which can lead to a reduction in anxiety symptoms.

Journaling can also be used to set goals and track progress in overcoming anxiety. Writing down specific goals, such as "I will reduce my worry about work by focusing on the present moment," can provide a sense of direction and motivation. By tracking progress over time, individuals can see how far they've come and celebrate their successes. This can be a powerful tool for building self-esteem and promoting feelings of self-efficacy.

It's also important to note that journaling is an accessible and low-cost tool for managing anxiety and can be done in the privacy of one's own home, which can be especially helpful for those who may feel hesitant to seek professional help.

2.2.2. Meditation

Meditation is an ancient practice that has been used for thousands of years to promote relaxation, reduce stress, and improve overall well-being. In recent years, research has been conducted to explore the effects of meditation on anxiety, and the findings have been quite promising.

Meditation is a non-pharmacological technique that aims to promote relaxation and reduce stress by encouraging the individual to focus their attention and eliminate the stream of thoughts that may be crowding their mind. There are various forms of meditation, including transcendental meditation, mindfulness meditation, and yoga-based meditation. Studies have shown that all of these forms of meditation can have a positive effect on anxiety.

One of the most well-established forms of meditation is mindfulness meditation. This technique involves paying attention to the present moment and accepting it without judgment. Mindfulness meditation has been shown to be effective in reducing symptoms of anxiety by helping individuals become more aware of their thoughts, emotions, and bodily sensations and to relate to them in a non-judgmental way. Mindfulness meditation also encourages individuals to adopt a more accepting attitude towards their experiences, which can help reduce anxiety symptoms.

The practice of mindfulness meditation involves sitting comfortably, focusing on the breath, and bringing one's attention to the present moment. When distracting thoughts arise, practitioners are instructed to acknowledge them and gently return their focus to the breath. This simple yet powerful practice can have a profound impact on the mind and body and has been shown to be effective in reducing symptoms of anxiety, depression, and stress.

By paying attention to the present moment, individuals can learn to recognize when their mind is dwelling on negative thoughts and emotions, and take steps to change their perspective. This can lead to a reduction in symptoms of anxiety and depression, as well as an improvement in overall well-being.

Mindfulness meditation can also improve physical health by reducing stress. Stress is known to have a negative impact on the body and has been linked to a range of health problems, such as heart disease, diabetes, and cancer. Mindfulness meditation has been shown to reduce the production of the stress hormone cortisol, which can lead to a reduction in physical symptoms of stress, such as high blood pressure and muscle tension.

Additionally, Mindfulness meditation can help to improve focus, concentration and memory. With regular practice, individuals can learn to focus their attention more effectively and can improve their ability to think clearly, which can be beneficial in both personal and professional settings.

It's important to note that mindfulness meditation is not a one-size-fits-all solution and that different individuals may experience different benefits. As with any practice, it takes time and consistent effort to see results, and it's important for individuals to find a practice that works for them.

Here is an easy mindfulness meditation script :

1. Find a quiet and comfortable space to sit. You can sit in a chair or cross-legged on the floor, whatever feels comfortable for you.

2. Close your eyes and take a deep breath in, counting to four as you inhale. Hold the breath for a count of four, and exhale for a count of four. Repeat this for a few rounds, paying attention to the sensation of your breath as you inhale and exhale.

3. Allow your breath to return to its natural rhythm without trying to control it.

4. Bring your attention to your body, starting from the top of your head and working your way down to your toes. Notice any areas of tension, and imagine breathing into these areas and releasing the tension with each exhale.

5. Bring your attention to your thoughts and notice them as they arise. Don't try to suppress them, just

observe them as they come and go, like clouds passing in the sky.

6. If your mind wanders and you get caught up in a thought, simply acknowledge it and gently return your attention to your breath.

7. Try to focus on the present moment without judgment, without getting caught up in thoughts about the past or the future.

8. Keep your attention on your breath as you continue to sit, observe and breathe.

9. As you become more comfortable with the meditation, you can increase the length of the practice, starting with short sessions of 5 minutes and working your way up to longer sessions.

10. When you feel ready, open your eyes and take a moment to re-orient yourself, feeling the calm and centeredness that you have created.

Remember that meditation is a practice, it may take time and some patience to get the hang of it, and it's not about reaching a specific state of mind but simply being present and aware of your thoughts, feelings, and bodily sensations in each moment. Give yourself the time and space to practice, without any expectations or pressure.

Transcendental meditation is another form of meditation that has been shown to be effective in reducing symptoms of anxiety. This technique involves the repetition of a word or phrase, which is thought to encourage a state of deep relaxation and inner peace. Research has shown that transcendental meditation can reduce anxiety symptoms by decreasing the activity of the sympathetic nervous system, which is responsible for the body's "fight or flight" response.

Here is an easy transcendental meditation script:

1. Find a quiet and comfortable place to sit where you will not be disturbed.
2. Close your eyes and take a few deep breaths, allowing your body to relax.
3. Choose a word or phrase that you will use as your "mantra," such as "peace" or "relax." This is a word or phrase that you will focus on during the meditation.

4. Begin to repeat your mantra silently to yourself. You can say it in your mind, or you can whisper it softly.

5. When your mind starts to wander and you find yourself thinking about other things, gently redirect your focus back to your mantra.

6. Continue repeating your mantra and focusing your mind on it for 10-20 minutes.

7. When you are finished, take a few deep breaths, open your eyes, and go about your day.

It is important to note that the whole point of transcendental meditation is to focus on your mantra and no other thing besides it. In the beginning, Your mind will wander, but with practice you will find it easier and easier to focus. It's also important to note that the effects of this type of meditation may not be immediate, but with regular practice, you may find that it helps to reduce stress, improve concentration and promote overall well-being.

Yoga-based meditation is a combination of physical postures, breathing exercises, and meditation. Yoga-based meditation can help to promote relaxation and reduce anxiety by reducing the activity of the sympathetic nervous system and increasing the activity of the parasympathetic nervous system, which is responsible for the "rest and digest" response. Practicing yoga regularly can improve anxiety-related symptoms, depression, and sleep.

Here is an easy yoga-based meditation script:

1. Find a quiet and comfortable place to sit or lie down where you will not be disturbed.
2. Begin by focusing on your breath. Take a few deep breaths in and out, feeling the rise and fall of your chest or the sensation of air moving through your nose.
3. Bring your attention to your body, starting at the top of your head and working your way down to your toes. Notice any areas of tension or discomfort, and breathe into those areas to help release them.
4. Next, bring your awareness to your lower belly, the area around your navel. As you breathe in, imagine

the breath filling up this area, expanding the belly outward. As you breathe out, imagine the breath emptying the belly, contracting it inward.

5. Continue to focus on your breath, following it as it moves in and out of the body. You can count your breath if it helps you to focus.

6. As you become more relaxed and your mind becomes more still, bring your attention to a point in your body, it can be your heart or third eye, where you can feel a sense of balance and peacefulness.

7. Stay here for several minutes, just breathing and feeling a sense of balance and peacefulness.

8. When you're ready, slowly open your eyes and go about your day.

You can play with the duration and breath count, but the main focus is to bring awareness to your breath and let your body relax. Yoga meditation is an ancient practice that can help to calm the mind and reduce stress. It can also help to improve overall well-being by aligning the body, mind and breath. It's also important to note that you can do this exercise in a seated position or standing position, the main objective is to bring awareness to the breath and the body and focus.

2.3. How to develop a deeper understanding of one's thoughts and feelings

Developing a deeper understanding of one's thoughts can be a challenging and ongoing process, but there are several techniques that can be used to help increase self-awareness and gain insight into one's thought patterns.

The two techniques mindfulness meditation and journaling, have already been mentioned.

Another method would be the practice of self-reflection. This can include set aside time each day, week, or month to reflect on oneself, one's actions and decisions and thoughts; this is a valuable way to increase self-awareness and gain insight into one's thoughts and emotions.

It could also include, therapy or counseling, where a person can talk through their thoughts with a trained professional. This can provide a safe and supportive space to process and explore one's thoughts and can also help to gain insight and perspective on patterns of thinking or behavior that may be impacting one's life.

Additionally, learning about different psychological concepts and theories can also be helpful in understanding one's thoughts and emotions. For instance, studying cognitive-behavioral theory can provide insight into how thoughts and behaviors are related, and can help to identify negative thought patterns that may be impacting one's well-being.

Overall, developing a deeper understanding of one's thoughts requires a combination of self-reflection, mindfulness, and other techniques and seeking professional help when necessary. It's important to remember that this process is ongoing and may require effort and time to truly gain deeper understanding of oneself.

3. Self-Care And Lifestyle Changes

3.1. The importance of self-care in managing anxiety

Self-care can include a variety of practices, such as exercise, healthy eating, getting enough sleep, and engaging in hobbies and activities that bring enjoyment.

Exercise is a crucial aspect of managing anxiety in men, as it helps to reduce stress and improve overall well-being. Anxiety is a common mental health condition that can have a significant impact on a person's life, and regular exercise can play an important role in managing its symptoms.

Physical activity has been found to have a positive effect on reducing anxiety symptoms. Exercise releases endorphins, also known as "feel-good" chemicals that can improve mood and reduce feelings of stress. Additionally, exercise can also improve sleep, and it has been found to be as effective as some medications for reducing symptoms of anxiety.

Exercise can also help to reduce the physical symptoms of anxiety such as muscle tension, racing heart and rapid breathing. Engaging in activities such as jogging, cycling, or weightlifting can help to release tension and reduce physical symptoms. Regular exercise can also help individuals to feel more in control of their body and mind, which can be particularly beneficial for people with anxiety.

Additionally, exercise can also be a useful tool for managing stress, which is a common trigger for anxiety. It has been found that engaging in regular physical activity can help to reduce stress by releasing tension and promoting relaxation. Exercise can also improve overall physical health and make people feel more capable and resilient in dealing with stressful situations.

Healthy eating is an important aspect of managing anxiety in men, as it can help to improve mood and reduce physical symptoms of anxiety. Anxiety is a common mental health condition that can have a significant impact on a person's life, and making sure to eat a balanced and nutritious diet can play a role in managing its symptoms.

A diet that is rich in fruits, vegetables, and whole grains can provide the necessary vitamins and minerals to maintain physical and mental well-being. These foods are also sources of antioxidants, which can help to protect against stress and promote relaxation. Additionally, consuming enough healthy fats and proteins can also be important in maintaining a balanced diet and supporting overall health, including mental health.

Eating a balanced diet can help to reduce inflammation in the body, which is a common contributor to anxiety and depression. Processed foods, refined sugars, and saturated fats have been linked to increased inflammation and can make anxiety symptoms worse. On the other hand, foods that are high in antioxidants, such as berries and leafy greens, can help to reduce inflammation and improve overall health.

A balanced diet also provides essential nutrients for the brain to function properly, specifically for neurotransmitters, which are chemical messengers in the brain that play a role in mood regulation. For example, foods high in omega-3 fatty acids, such as fish, walnuts and flaxseeds, are essential for the production of serotonin, a neurotransmitter that can affect mood and anxiety symptoms.

It is also worth noting that regular eating patterns can also play a role in managing anxiety; skipping meals or going too long without eating can cause blood sugar levels to drop, which can lead to feelings of anxiety and irritability. Therefore, it is important to maintain regular eating habits and try to eat a balanced diet throughout the day.

In conclusion, healthy eating is an important aspect of managing anxiety in men, as it can help to improve mood, reduce physical symptoms of anxiety, reduce inflammation and provide essential nutrients for the brain to function properly. Eating a balanced and nutritious diet can provide a foundation for good physical and mental health, and can be a useful tool for managing anxiety symptoms. It is essential for men to pay attention to their diet, especially when they are struggling with anxiety, to improve their mental and physical well-being.

Getting enough sleep is an important aspect of managing anxiety in men, as it can help to reduce stress and improve overall well-being. Anxiety is a common mental health condition that can have a significant impact on a person's life, and making sure to get enough sleep can play a role in managing its symptoms.

Sleep plays a vital role in regulating mood and reducing stress. A lack of sleep can make anxiety symptoms worse and can also increase the risk of developing anxiety disorders. When the body is tired, it is harder to cope with stressors, and the mind is less able to think clearly and calmly, which can make it harder to manage anxious thoughts and feelings.

Additionally, getting enough sleep can help to regulate the release of hormones in the body, such as cortisol, which is often referred to as the "stress hormone." Elevated levels of cortisol can contribute to feelings of anxiety and irritability. Getting enough sleep can help to regulate the release of cortisol and other hormones, which can help to reduce symptoms of anxiety.

Quality of sleep is also important. Individuals should aim for a consistent sleep schedule and sleep environment. This includes setting a regular bedtime, avoiding screens and stimulating activities before bed, and creating a comfortable and dark sleep environment.

It is also important to note that men may have a harder time reaching out for help when it comes to mental health concerns, and sleep is an accessible form of self-care and stress management. Prioritizing sleep can help men to maintain good mental health and reduce symptoms of anxiety.

In conclusion, getting enough sleep is an important aspect of managing anxiety in men, as it can help to reduce stress, improve overall well-being, and regulate the release of hormones in the body. Establishing a regular sleep schedule and a comfortable sleep environment, in addition to paying attention to sleep quality, is key in managing anxiety symptoms. It is essential for men to make sure they get enough sleep, especially when they are struggling with anxiety, to improve their mental and physical well-being.

Engaging in hobbies and activities that bring enjoyment is an important aspect of managing anxiety in men, as it can help to reduce stress and improve overall well-being. Anxiety is a common mental health condition that can have a significant impact on a person's life, and engaging in enjoyable activities can play a role in managing its symptoms.

Participating in activities that bring enjoyment, such as hobbies, can be a useful tool for managing stress, which is a common trigger for anxiety. When people engage in activities that they enjoy, it can take their minds off of their worries, provide a sense of accomplishment, and boost their self-esteem. This can be beneficial in managing symptoms of anxiety and promoting relaxation.

Additionally, hobbies and activities can provide a sense of purpose and meaning. Often anxiety and depression can be related to a feeling of lack of control and purpose; engaging in activities that bring enjoyment can provide a sense of mastery, autonomy, and self-determination which can lead to increased feelings of control and well-being.

It is important to note that hobbies can vary from person to person, and it's important for men to find activities that they personally find enjoyable. This can include sports, playing musical instruments, reading, cooking, hiking, photography, or any other activity that brings a sense of pleasure and enjoyment. For example, for some men, participating in a sport can provide a sense of accomplishment and camaraderie, while for others, reading or writing can provide a sense of relaxation and solitude.

It is also worth noting that hobbies and activities can also be a form of self-care and stress management, especially for men who may have a harder time seeking help for mental health concerns. Engaging in activities that bring enjoyment can be a healthy way to cope with stress and anxiety, and to improve overall well-being.

In conclusion, engaging in hobbies and activities that bring enjoyment is an important aspect of managing anxiety in men, as it can help to reduce stress, improve overall well-being, and provide a sense of purpose and meaning. It is essential for men to find hobbies and activities that they personally enjoy and make them a regular part of their lives, especially when they are struggling with anxiety. By engaging in activities that bring enjoyment, men can learn to manage their symptoms and live fulfilling lives despite the presence of anxiety.

3.2. Facing things

Before moving on to improvements in life styles, I figured it would be essential to mention the importance of facing things. The importance of moving straightforward on the path you know you have to take.

When an individual avoids a situation or thing that causes them anxiety, they are not giving themselves the opportunity to learn how to cope with their feelings. Instead, they are reinforcing the idea that the situation or thing is something to be feared. This creates a cycle of anxiety where the individual becomes more and more afraid of the situation or thing, leading to more avoidance, which in turn leads to more anxiety and fear.

Furthermore, avoidance can lead to difficulty in daily functioning. When an individual avoids a certain situation or thing, they may be limiting their ability to live their life to the fullest. Someone with social anxiety may avoid social situations, which can limit their ability to make friends and interact with others.

Avoiding anxiety can also lead to a loss of opportunities. For example, someone with a fear of public speaking may avoid giving presentations or speeches, which can limit their career advancement opportunities.

Facing things head-on can also lead to increased self-esteem and self-confidence. When an individual avoids a situation or thing, they may feel like they are not capable of handling it. On the other hand, when an individual faces a situation or thing, they are showing themselves that they are capable of handling it. This can lead to increased self-esteem and self-confidence, which can positively impact all areas of life.

Facing things can help bring a sense of control over one's life. When an individual avoids a certain situation or thing, they may feel like they are at the mercy of their fear. On the other hand, when an individual faces their fear, they are taking control of their life. They are showing themselves that they have the power to overcome their fear and that they are in control of their life.

It is important to note that avoidance is not always a bad thing. Sometimes, it is necessary to avoid a situation or thing that is causing excessive anxiety. However, it is important to understand that avoiding anxiety is not a long-term solution. The key is to learn how to cope with anxiety and face it head-on. This can be done through therapy, mindfulness, and other coping strategies.

3.3. Tips for improving sleep, diet, and exercise

As mentioned before, many little incremental changes are necessary to establish an anxiety-free life. I collected the most important tips in each of the fields of sleep, diet and exercise.

3.3.1. List Of Tips To Improve Sleep:

1. Establish a regular sleep schedule by going to bed and waking up at the same time every day.

2. Create a comfortable and dark sleep environment, including comfortable bedding and a room temperature that feels comfortable to you.

3. Avoid screens, such as smartphones, tablets, and televisions, for at least an hour before bed.

4. Avoid caffeine, nicotine, and alcohol close to bedtime.

5. Try relaxation techniques such as deep breathing, meditation, or yoga to help calm your mind and prepare for sleep.

6. Make sure your mattress and pillow are comfortable and provide enough support.

7. Use earplugs or a white noise machine to block out any distracting sounds that may disrupt your sleep.

8. Take a warm bath or shower before bedtime to help relax your muscles and prepare your body for sleep.

9. Try to avoid heavy meals, and don't go to bed hungry, but also avoid eating too close to bedtime.

10. Keep your bedroom cool, as the ideal temperature for sleeping is around 60-67 degrees Fahrenheit.

11. Establish a pre-sleep routine, such as reading a book or practicing relaxation exercises.

12. Use light-blocking curtains or an eye mask to block out any unwanted light in your bedroom.

13. Get regular exercise, but avoid strenuous activity close to bedtime.

14. Use comfortable and breathable pajamas.

15. Practice mindfulness and try to focus on the present moment before bed, avoiding worry about the past or future

16. Invest in a good quality mattress and pillows

17. Consider the use of a sleep-tracking app, to monitor sleep pattern and detect any issues.

18. Use natural supplements such as melatonin, but only under the guidance of your health care professional.

19. Consider aromatherapy, with scents such as lavender and chamomile to promote relaxation.

20. Make sure your room is quiet and dark enough, to provide a peaceful and calming atmosphere for sleep.

3.3.2. List of Tips To Improve Diet And Reduce Anxiety:

1. Incorporate more fruits, vegetables, and whole grains into your diet. These foods are rich in vitamins and minerals that can help to promote overall health and well-being.

2. Limit processed foods, refined sugars, and saturated fats, as they have been linked to increased inflammation and can make anxiety symptoms worse.

3. Increase your intake of foods high in omega-3 fatty acids, such as fish, walnuts, and flaxseeds, as these are essential for the production of neurotransmitters that affect mood and anxiety.

4. Avoid caffeine, as it can increase feelings of anxiety and disrupt sleep.

5. Drink plenty of water, as dehydration can lead to feelings of irritability and anxiety.

6. Incorporate more probiotics-rich food like yogurt, kefir, kimchi, and sauerkraut, as they help with gut health and in turn, promote healthy brain function.

7. Avoid skipping meals or going too long without eating, as this can cause blood sugar levels to drop, leading to feelings of anxiety and irritability.

8. Consider incorporating adaptogens, like ashwagandha, which are natural herbs that help the body to cope with stress.

9. Consume Vitamin B-rich food, such as green leafy vegetables, fish, and eggs, as they help to regulate the nervous system and improve mood.

10. Incorporate more magnesium-rich foods, such as almonds, spinach, and black beans, as magnesium can help to reduce feelings of anxiety.

11. Consider incorporating a balanced ratio of macronutrients (carbs, proteins, and fats) to keep blood sugar levels stable and steady.

12. Reduce your alcohol intake, as alcohol can worsen anxiety symptoms.

13. Try to eat slowly and mindfully, paying attention to the taste and texture of your food.

14. Try to eat a balanced diet, with a variety of foods to provide a balance of nutrients.

15. consider trying a low-inflammation diet, which typically includes an increase of anti-inflammatory foods and a decrease of processed and refined foods.

16. Keep a food diary, to monitor how certain foods may affect your mood and anxiety levels.

3.3.3. List of Tips To Reduce Anxiety With Exercise:

1. Incorporate regular aerobic exercises such as running, cycling, or swimming, as it can help reduce anxiety symptoms by releasing endorphins, also known as "feel-good" chemicals.

2. Engage in strength training, as it can help to reduce muscle tension and physical symptoms of anxiety.

3. Consider trying yoga, as it has been found to be effective in reducing symptoms of anxiety by promoting relaxation and calm.

4. Make sure to choose activities you enjoy, as it will increase the chances of sticking to an exercise routine.

5. Set realistic goals, such as starting with a small amount of exercise time and gradually increasing it.

6. Establish a regular exercise routine, by scheduling it in your calendar, like any other appointment.

7. Expose yourself to the natural environment by going for a walk or run outside, as it can help to reduce feelings of stress and anxiety.

8. Take up a team sport to get the added benefit of social interaction and camaraderie.

9. Try to exercise at the same time every day to develop a habit, and if possible, try to exercise in the morning to set a positive tone for the day.

10. Make sure to warm up before starting your exercise routine, to prevent injury and prepare your body for physical activity.

11. Listen to your body and adjust your exercise routine as needed, taking rest days if you feel fatigued or ill.

12. Incorporate a mix of cardio and strength training into your exercise routine for optimal benefits.

13. Incorporate stretching and flexibility exercises, as they can help to release muscle tension and promote relaxation.

14. Get a workout buddy, or join a class or a team to increase accountability and social support.

15. Use music or podcast during your workout to distract your mind and make the time pass more quickly.

16. Track your progress, whether by using a fitness tracker or a journal, it can help to boost your motivation and self-esteem.

17. Make sure to cool down after your exercise routine by stretching or walking for a few

3.4. How to create a balanced and healthy lifestyle that supports mental well-being

Creating a schedule that works and establishing new habits are essential steps in achieving personal goals and leading a fulfilling life. These two elements go hand in hand as a schedule can help to structure the day and provide a framework for creating new habits. Here are some tips for men on how to make a schedule that works and how to create new habits.

First, it's important to start by setting clear goals. Having a specific and measurable goal in mind can help to provide direction and motivation when creating a schedule and establishing new habits. Make sure to set realistic goals, and break them down into smaller, more manageable tasks.

Second, create a schedule that fits with your lifestyle. Take into consideration any recurring obligations or commitments and factor them into your schedule. Be realistic about how much time you have available, and don't overbook yourself.

Third, prioritize your tasks and activities. Not all tasks and activities are created equal, and it's important to focus on the most important tasks first. This will help to ensure that you are making the most efficient use of your time.

Fourth, use a calendar or planner to schedule your tasks and activities. Having a visual representation of your schedule can help to keep you on track and make it easier to stay organized.

Fifth, when creating new habits, it is important to start small, making a habit that is easy to start with, and gradually building on it. A good rule of thumb is to start with a habit that can be accomplished in less than 2 minutes. When it becomes a habit and easy to maintain, add another small habit until you reach your goal.

Sixth, be consistent and persistent. Habits are formed by repeating actions over time; consistency is key. If a schedule or habit is repeatedly ignored, it will be difficult to maintain, so try to stick with it, even when it becomes difficult.

Seventh, Hold yourself accountable for your actions. Keep track of your progress, review it regularly, and don't celebrate all your wins. And remember, it's okay to slip up, don't beat yourself up. Get back on track as soon as you can.

In summary, creating a schedule that works and establishing new habits can help to improve productivity and overall well-being. Start by setting clear goals, creating a schedule that fits your lifestyle, prioritizing tasks, using a calendar or planner, starting small and building on success, being consistent and persistent, and holding yourself accountable. With these tips, men can take steps to achieve their goals and lead more fulfilling life.

4. Cognitive-Behavioral Therapy (CBT)

4.1. An overview of CBT, a widely used therapy for anxiety disorders

Cognitive-behavioral therapy (CBT) is a widely used therapy for treating anxiety disorders. CBT is a form of talk therapy that focuses on the connection between thoughts, feelings, and behaviors. The theory behind CBT is that our thoughts, beliefs, and attitudes can affect our emotions and behaviors. When we have negative thoughts or beliefs, they can lead to negative emotions such as anxiety. The goal of CBT is to help individuals recognize and change these negative thoughts and beliefs in order to reduce their anxiety symptoms.

CBT typically involves working with a therapist on a regular basis, usually once a week for several months.

During therapy sessions, the therapist will help the individual identify patterns in their thoughts, feelings, and behaviors that are contributing to their anxiety. Together, they will work to identify and challenge negative thoughts and beliefs, as well as develop new, more positive ways of thinking. The therapist may also provide the individual with tools and strategies for managing anxiety symptoms, such as relaxation techniques, problem-solving, and exposure therapy.

One key component of CBT is cognitive restructuring. This is the process of identifying and changing negative thoughts and beliefs that are contributing to anxiety. This may involve learning to recognize and challenge thoughts that are unrealistic or irrational, such as "I'm going to fail" or "I'm going to have a panic attack." The therapist will help the individual to reframe these thoughts in a more positive and realistic way, such as "I've succeeded in the past, and I can do it again" or "I can manage my panic attacks by using the techniques I've learned."

Another important component of CBT is exposure therapy. This involves gradually exposing the individual to the things or situations that they fear, in a controlled and safe environment, such as gradually facing a phobia by visualizing it, then looking at pictures of it, going near the place, etc. This can help the individual to learn that their fears are not as dangerous as they thought and that they have the ability to cope with them.

CBT is a well-established and highly effective treatment for a variety of anxiety disorders, including generalized anxiety disorder, panic disorder, social anxiety disorder, and specific phobias. Research has shown that CBT can be as effective as medication in treating anxiety disorders and that the benefits of CBT can continue long after therapy has ended.

CBT is also widely adapted and flexible; it can be done in individual or group settings, face-to-face or via videoconferencing, and has been used with a variety of populations, including children and older adults.

In conclusion, Cognitive-behavioral therapy (CBT) is a highly effective form of talk therapy for treating anxiety disorders. CBT helps individuals recognize and change negative thoughts and beliefs that are contributing to their anxiety, as well as develop new, more positive ways of thinking. By working with a therapist and learning the strategies of cognitive restructuring and exposure therapy, individuals can learn to manage their anxiety symptoms and lead a happier, more fulfilling life.

There was a friend of mine named Tom who was skeptical about psychotherapy. He had always believed that people should be able to solve their own problems and that therapy was for weak-minded individuals. However, he was struggling with anxiety and depression, and despite his best efforts, he couldn't seem to shake them.

Tom had always been a perfectionist, and this trait of his led to a lot of stress in his work and personal life. He would often get stuck in a cycle of negative thoughts, thinking he was not good enough and that he was going to fail. His anxiety and depression were getting in the way of him being able to enjoy life, and he knew that he needed to do something about it.

He decided to give cognitive-behavioral therapy (CBT) a try. Despite his skepticism, he was willing to give it a chance because he was desperate to feel better. He began by searching for a therapist who specialized in CBT and eventually found one whom he felt comfortable working with.

The first step of CBT is to identify and understand the negative thoughts and beliefs that contribute to a person's problems. Tom's therapist helped him to understand that his thoughts were not always accurate and that they were often an exaggeration of the truth. Together, they worked on identifying his negative thought patterns and challenging them with evidence from reality.

Tom was resistant at first, as he believed that his thoughts were entirely accurate and reasonable. However, as he began to understand the impact that his thoughts were having on his mood and behavior, he became more open to the idea of changing his perspective.

They worked on challenging his thoughts by questioning his assumptions and looking for alternative explanations to what he was thinking. Tom learned to focus on the present moment and not get too caught up in the future or the past. He also learned to use techniques like breathing exercises, mindfulness, and positive self-talk to help reduce his anxiety and depression.

Slowly but surely, Tom began to feel better. His anxiety and depression began to lift, and he found that he was able to enjoy life more fully. He realized that therapy had been a valuable experience and that his initial skepticism was completely unfounded. He had learned a lot about himself, his thoughts, and his feelings, and he felt like a new man.

Tom's story shows that sometimes, even the most skeptical people can benefit from therapy. With the right therapist and an open mind, it is possible to overcome negative thoughts and emotions and lead a happier and more fulfilling life.

4.2. Finding the right therapist

Finding the right therapist can be a difficult and daunting task. It can be hard to know where to start, and the process of searching for a therapist can be a source of stress and anxiety in and of itself. However, it is important to remember that the right therapist is out there, and the benefits of therapy are well worth the effort it takes to find them.

When looking for a therapist, it is important to do your research. You can start by talking to your primary care doctor for recommendations or by searching online for therapists in your area. Reading reviews from other people who have seen the therapist can also be helpful. It can be helpful to look for a therapist who specializes in the specific issue you are dealing with, such as anxiety or depression.

Online psychotherapy, also known as teletherapy or e-therapy, is the delivery of mental health services via the internet. This includes a variety of forms, such as video conferencing, phone calls, and messaging.

One of the main benefits of online psychotherapy is convenience. Clients can receive therapy from the comfort of their own home without the need to travel to a physical location. This can be especially beneficial for those who live in remote areas or have mobility issues. Additionally, online therapy can be less expensive than in-person therapy, as it eliminates the need for office space and other overhead costs.

Another benefit of online psychotherapy is the ability to connect with a wider range of therapists. Traditional therapy often requires clients to find a therapist within their local area, but with online therapy, clients have access to a much larger pool of therapists from all over the world. This can be especially helpful for those seeking specialized treatment or for those who may not feel comfortable with a therapist in their local area.

Online psychotherapy can also be beneficial for those who may feel more comfortable communicating through technology rather than in-person. For example, some people may have social anxiety and may feel more comfortable sharing their thoughts and feelings through messaging or video conferencing rather than in-person.

Despite the benefits, there are some concerns about the effectiveness of online psychotherapy. One concern is that therapy delivered remotely may not be as effective as in-person therapy. However, research has found that online therapy can be just as effective as in-person therapy in treating a variety of conditions, such as anxiety and depression. Another concern is that therapy delivered remotely may not be as secure as in-person therapy. It's important to ensure that the platform being used is secure and that the therapist is licensed and reputable.

Once you have a list of potential therapists, whether online or locally, it can be helpful to call or email them to ask about their availability and to get a sense of whether you think they would be a good fit. Some people find it helpful to schedule an initial consultation to meet with the therapist in person and ask any questions they may have before committing to a full course of therapy.

It can be frustrating to go through the process of searching for a therapist, and it is not uncommon to feel discouraged if you haven't found the right therapist right away. However, it is important to remember that finding the right therapist is a process and that it may take some time and perseverance to find the right person.

It is also important to remember that it's not uncommon that the first therapist might not be the right fit and that it's okay to keep searching and try another one. It may take some trial and error, but it is essential to find a therapist whom you feel comfortable with and who can help you effectively address the issues you are dealing with.

It's essential to remember that having the belief that therapy is important is essential. Therapy can be incredibly helpful in treating a wide range of mental health issues, including anxiety and depression. It can help people to better understand themselves, to manage their thoughts and emotions, and to make positive changes in their lives. It can also provide them with the tools and skills they need to cope with future challenges.

In conclusion, finding the right therapist takes time and effort, but it's an important step in improving one's mental health. The process of searching for a therapist can be challenging, but with perseverance and belief in the importance of therapy, people can find the right therapist and can reap the many benefits that therapy has to offer. It's a process of self-discovery, self-improvement, and growth. It's the first step of a journey that requires courage and an open mind.

4.3. How to reframe thoughts in a more positive and empowering way

Reframing thoughts is a technique used in cognitive-behavioral therapy to help individuals change negative and unhelpful thinking patterns. By reframing, individuals can change the way they look at a situation, which can ultimately change their emotional response to it. Here are some steps to help reframe thoughts in a more positive and empowering way:

1. Identify the negative thought. The first step in reframing is to recognize when you have a negative thought. Be mindful of your thoughts

and pay attention when you are feeling down or upset.

2. Challenge the thought. Once you have identified the negative thought, ask yourself if it is based on fact or just your perception of the situation. Are you jumping to conclusions, or are there other explanations for the event?

3. Look for the positive. Instead of focusing solely on the negative, try to find a positive aspect of the situation. Are there any opportunities or lessons to be learned?

4. Reframe the thought. Using the positive aspect of the situation, rephrase the negative thought in a more empowering and positive way.

5. Repeat the new thought. Repeat the reframed thought to yourself, allowing it to become ingrained in your mind.

It's important to keep in mind that reframing thoughts takes practice, and it's not always possible to have a positive outlook on everything, but with time and patience, it can become a natural part of your thought process. Additionally, it is also helpful to try and engage in activities you enjoy, be around positive people, take care of your physical and emotional well-being and focus on things you are grateful for; all of these will give you a positive outlook and a more empowering way of thinking.

It's worth noting that while reframing thoughts is a useful tool, it's not the only one, and it's not going to work every time; other techniques, such as mindfulness, problem-solving, and relaxation techniques, can be really helpful in managing negative thoughts, feelings, and emotions as well.

5. Alternative Therapies

5.1. Overview of alternative therapies for anxiety, such as acupuncture, aromatherapy, and yoga

Anxiety is a common mental health condition that affects millions of people. While traditional therapies such as counseling and medication are effective for many people, some people may prefer to use alternative therapies to manage their anxiety. Here is an overview of a few alternative therapies that have been used to treat anxiety:

1. Acupuncture: Acupuncture is a traditional Chinese medicine practice that involves the insertion of thin needles into specific points of the body. It is believed to balance the body's energy, or qi, and promote healing. Research has shown that acupuncture may be effective in reducing symptoms of anxiety and depression.

2. Aromatherapy: Aromatherapy involves the use of essential oils to promote relaxation and well-being. Different essential oils have different properties and can be used for different purposes. Some common essential oils used for anxiety include lavender, peppermint, and bergamot. Aromatherapy can be used through massage, inhaling the oils, or using a diffuser.

3. Yoga: Yoga is a mind-body practice that combines physical postures, breathing exercises, and meditation. Research has shown that yoga can be

effective in reducing anxiety and stress. Yoga can work by reducing muscle tension and promoting relaxation, as well as by changing the way an individual thinks and feels about their thoughts and experiences.

4. Mindfulness: Mindfulness practices like mindfulness-based stress reduction (MBSR) and mindfulness-based cognitive therapy (MBCT) are gaining popularity in recent years as a form of treatment for anxiety and depression. These practices are based on being present at the moment and focusing on observing thoughts, emotions, and body sensations without judgment.

5. Herbal Remedies: Some herbs, such as Kava, passionflower, and valerian root, have been traditionally used for centuries for their calming effects and have been studied for their effectiveness in reducing anxiety symptoms. They should be used under professional guidance as they may interact with medications and should be taken in recommended doses and for a limited time.

It's worth noting that alternative therapies may not be appropriate for everyone and should be used in conjunction with traditional therapies. Consultation with a healthcare professional is important before trying any alternative therapies for anxiety to ensure that it's safe for you and to understand the possible risks and benefits of each method.

5.2. Information on supplements and natural remedies that may help reduce anxiety

Omega-3 fatty acids, magnesium, L-Theanine, valerian root, passionflower, kava, and ashwagandha are all-natural remedies and supplements that have been shown to help reduce symptoms of anxiety.

Magnesium is a mineral that plays a critical role in many bodily functions, including the regulation of nerve and muscle function. Recent research has shown that low levels of magnesium may be associated with increased symptoms of anxiety. This has led to the suggestion that supplementing with magnesium may be a useful strategy for reducing anxiety.

One way that magnesium may help to reduce anxiety is by regulating the activity of neurotransmitters, which are chemical messengers in the brain that play a key role in regulating mood and emotions. Magnesium has been shown to modulate the activity of several neurotransmitters, including GABA, which is known to have a calming effect on the brain. By increasing the activity of GABA, magnesium may help to reduce feelings of anxiety and promote relaxation.

Magnesium can also help to reduce anxiety by regulating the HPA (hypothalamic-pituitary-adrenal) axis, which is a complex system that regulates the body's response to stress. Research has shown that low levels of magnesium can disrupt the HPA axis and contribute to the development of anxiety. By restoring normal function to the HPA axis, magnesium may help to reduce anxiety symptoms.

Additionally, magnesium can also help to improve sleep, one of the factors that can contribute to anxiety, People who have anxiety often report difficulty sleeping, and magnesium has been found to be helpful in improving sleep quality. This is one of the reasons it's often used as a sleep aid.

It's worth noting that not all forms of magnesium are the same, some forms are better absorbed by the body than others, and different forms may have different effects on anxiety. Some forms of magnesium that are well-absorbed include magnesium citrate, magnesium glycinate, and magnesium threonate. Also, magnesium supplements can have possible side effects such as diarrhea and stomach discomfort. Therefore it's always best to talk to a healthcare professional before supplementing with magnesium to ensure that it's safe and appropriate for you.

In conclusion, magnesium is a mineral that plays a critical role in many bodily functions, including the regulation of nerve and muscle function. Low levels of magnesium may be associated with increased symptoms of anxiety, and supplementing with magnesium may be a useful strategy for reducing anxiety by modulating neurotransmitters, regulating the HPA axis, and improving sleep. However, it's important to consult with a healthcare professional before taking magnesium supplements to ensure that it's safe and appropriate for you.

L-Theanine is an amino acid that is commonly found in green tea leaves. It is known for its ability to promote relaxation and reduce feelings of stress and anxiety. Research has shown that L-Theanine can help to reduce symptoms of anxiety by modulating the activity of certain neurotransmitters in the brain.

One of the ways L-Theanine may help reduce anxiety is by increasing the activity of the neurotransmitter GABA, which is known to have a calming effect on the brain. GABA plays an important role in regulating the activity of neurons in the brain and has been shown to be involved in the development of anxiety. By increasing the activity of GABA, L-Theanine may help to reduce feelings of anxiety and promote relaxation.

Another way L-Theanine may help reduce anxiety is by decreasing the activity of the neurotransmitter glutamate, which is known to be involved in the development of anxiety. Glutamate is an excitatory neurotransmitter, and too much of it can lead to feelings of anxiety and restlessness. L-Theanine is able to decrease the activity of glutamate, resulting in a reduction of feelings of anxiety.

L-Theanine also helps to increase the levels of serotonin and dopamine in the brain, two neurotransmitters that are known to play a role in regulating mood and emotions. These neurotransmitters are known to be involved in the development of anxiety, and by increasing their levels, L-Theanine may help to reduce feelings of anxiety.

Furthermore, L-Theanine has been found to have an effect on the alpha brain waves, which are associated with a state of relaxed alertness and are known to be involved in the development of anxiety. It promotes the production of these waves, which may help to reduce feelings of anxiety and promote relaxation.

It's worth noting that L-Theanine is considered to be safe with minimal side effects and can be consumed in supplement form or as part of a cup of green tea. However, as with any supplement, it's important to talk to a healthcare professional before taking it, especially if you're on medication or if you have any underlying medical condition.

In conclusion, L-Theanine is an amino acid that is commonly found in green tea leaves and is known for its ability to promote relaxation and reduce feelings of stress and anxiety. Research has shown that L-Theanine can help reduce anxiety by modulating the activity of certain neurotransmitters in the brain, including GABA, glutamate, serotonin, and dopamine, and by promoting the production of alpha brain waves. It is considered safe with minimal side effects and can be consumed in supplement form or as part of a cup of green tea; however, always best to consult with a healthcare professional before taking it.

Valerian root is an herb used for centuries to promote relaxation and reduce anxiety. It is commonly used as a natural remedy for insomnia, as well as for anxiety disorders such as generalized anxiety disorder (GAD) and social anxiety disorder (SAD).

Valerian root is believed to work by increasing the levels of a neurotransmitter called GABA in the brain. GABA is an inhibitory neurotransmitter, which means it helps to calm the activity of the brain. By increasing the levels of GABA, valerian root may help reduce anxiety and promote relaxation.

Valerian root also contains compounds known as valerenic acids and valepotriates; these compounds have been found to have a calming effect and have been found to have sedative properties. Studies have shown that valerian root can help to reduce symptoms of anxiety, such as restlessness, irritability, and tension.

Valerian root can also improve sleep quality, and anxious people often report difficulty sleeping. Valerian root has been found to be helpful in improving sleep quality by reducing the time it takes to fall asleep and by increasing the amount of time spent in deep sleep. Improving sleep quality can help reduce anxiety and improve overall well-being.

Valerian root can be consumed in the form of capsules, tinctures, teas, or dried root. It is considered safe when used as directed, but it can cause some side effects, such as drowsiness, dizziness, and headache. Therefore, it's important to talk to a healthcare professional before taking valerian root, especially if you're taking medication or have any underlying medical conditions.

In conclusion, valerian root is an herb that has been used for centuries to promote relaxation and reduce anxiety. It is believed to work by increasing the levels of GABA in the brain and by containing compounds known as valerenic acids and valepotriates, which have calming effects and sedative properties. It can also improve sleep quality, reducing the time it takes to fall asleep, and increasing the amount of time spent in deep sleep. It is considered safe when used as directed, but always best to consult with a healthcare professional before taking valerian root.

Passionflower, kava, and ashwagandha are all natural remedies traditionally used to reduce anxiety and promote relaxation. Each of these remedies works in different ways to help reduce anxiety, and research has shown that they can be effective in reducing symptoms of anxiety.

Passionflower is an herb that has been used for centuries to treat anxiety and insomnia. It contains compounds that are believed to have a calming effect on the nervous system. For example, Passionflower has been found to increase the levels of GABA, which is a neurotransmitter that helps to calm the brain; this can help to reduce feelings of anxiety and promote relaxation. Additionally, Passionflower has been found to have a mild sedative effect that can help promote sleep, which is often disrupted in people with anxiety.

Kava is a traditional herb that has been used for centuries to reduce anxiety and promote relaxation. It contains compounds called kavalactones, believed to have a calming effect on the nervous system. Kava has been found to be effective in reducing symptoms of anxiety, such as restlessness and irritability. It also can help to promote sleep and reduce insomnia. However, it's worth mentioning that kava has been associated with rare cases of liver injury, which might limit its use in some countries.

Ashwagandha is an Ayurvedic herb that has been traditionally used to reduce stress and anxiety. It is believed to work by reducing the activity of the stress hormone cortisol, which can contribute to the development of anxiety. It also helps to regulate the activity of neurotransmitters such as serotonin and dopamine, which play a key role in regulating mood and emotions. Studies have found that ashwagandha can effectively reduce anxiety symptoms, including feelings of restlessness and irritability.

It's worth noting that each of these remedies may not be appropriate for everyone and should be used in conjunction with traditional therapies. Additionally, it's important to consult with a healthcare professional before taking any supplements or natural remedies, as they may interact with any medications you take or have any adverse effects. It's also important to ensure the products are sourced from reputable manufacturers to guarantee the purity and quality of the product.

Discussion of the potential benefits and drawbacks of these therapies

Alternative anxiety therapies refer to treatments that are not considered to be part of conventional Western medicine, such as herbal remedies, acupuncture, mindfulness, and yoga. These therapies may offer a range of potential benefits for people with anxiety, such as:

1. Non-invasive: Alternative anxiety therapies are generally non-invasive and do not involve drugs or surgery. This can make them an appealing option for people who are looking for a more natural approach to treating their anxiety.

2. Low risk of side effects: Some alternative therapies may have fewer side effects than traditional medication, which can be especially beneficial for individuals who cannot tolerate certain medications or have an aversion to them.

3. Addresses root causes: Many alternative therapies aim to address the root causes of anxiety rather than just managing symptoms. For example, acupuncture may help to balance the body's energy, while yoga and mindfulness practices focus on addressing underlying stress, tension, and negative thoughts.

4. Integrative approach: Alternative therapies can be integrated with traditional therapies, such as counseling or medication, to enhance the effectiveness of treatment. This is called an integrative approach, which aims to address the holistic needs of the individual and provide a personalized treatment plan.

5. Empowerment: Alternative therapies often involve active participation and learning new techniques, which can be empowering for individuals who have a

sense of control over their treatment and their symptoms.

6. Addresses mind-body connection: Alternative therapies, such as Yoga, meditation, and mindfulness, focus on the mind-body connection; they aim to help an individual develop an understanding of how their thoughts, emotions, and physical sensations are interconnected and how to manage them.

7. Cost-effective: Alternative therapies may be more cost effective for some people when compared to traditional therapy and medication.

8. While alternative anxiety therapies may offer a range of potential benefits, there are also some potential drawbacks to consider. These include:

9. Limited scientific evidence: While some alternative therapies, such as acupuncture and yoga, have been the subject of scientific research, the evidence supporting their effectiveness in treating anxiety is still limited. Some alternative therapies lack rigorous scientific research to support their claims.

10. Lack of regulation: Many alternative therapies are not regulated by government agencies, which means that their safety and effectiveness may need to be fully understood. Products may not have consistent quality and purity.

11. Lack of standardization: The dosage and method of administration of alternative therapies can vary widely, which makes it difficult to know how much of the treatment is needed for it to be effective and if it's safe.

12. Interaction with other treatments: Alternative therapies may interact with other medications or treatments, which could cause harmful side effects or compromise the effectiveness of the treatment.

13. Incompatibility with certain individuals: Some alternative therapies may not be suitable for individuals with certain health conditions or allergies. For example, a therapy that involves certain herbs or supplements may not be suitable for people with certain health conditions or allergies.

14. Inadequate supervision: Alternative therapies, such as herbal remedies, self-help books, or online

programs, may not provide adequate supervision, which could put people who are already struggling with anxiety at risk of further harm.

While alternative anxiety therapies may offer a range of potential benefits, they may also have potential drawbacks. It is important to consult with a healthcare professional to evaluate the appropriateness and safety of alternative therapy in each case. They can help to weigh the risks and benefits and help determine if an alternative therapy is an appropriate course of action for treating an individual's anxiety.

6. Social Support & Connection

6.1. The importance of social support and connection in managing anxiety

Social support and connection are crucial factors in managing anxiety. Studies have shown that individuals with strong social support networks have lower levels of anxiety and depression compared to those who lack social connections. This is because social support can provide a sense of belonging and validation, which can help to counteract feelings of isolation and self-doubt.

One way that social support can help to manage anxiety is by providing a sounding board for worries and concerns. When individuals feel anxious, they may have racing thoughts and overwhelming worry. Having someone to talk to about these feelings can help to put things into perspective and provide a sense of validation and understanding.

Additionally, social connections can also provide a sense of safety and security. When individuals feel anxious, they may feel as if they are in danger or that something bad is going to happen. Having people in their lives whom they can rely on can help to counteract these feelings of fear and uncertainty.

Furthermore, social support can also be a source of distraction and diversion from anxious thoughts. Spending time with friends and family, engaging in hobbies and activities, and participating in group therapy can all provide a sense of normalcy and routine, which can help to reduce feelings of anxiety.

Being a "lone wolf" or wanting to achieve everything alone can have both benefits and drawbacks.

One benefit of being a lone wolf is that individuals who choose this path may have a strong sense of self-reliance and independence. They may be able to achieve their goals without relying on others, which can be empowering and lead to a sense of accomplishment. Additionally, they may be less likely to be influenced by the opinions and actions of others, which can lead to a greater sense of authenticity and self-expression.

Another benefit of being a lone wolf is that individuals may have more control over their own lives and decisions. They may not have to rely on others for support, which can lead to a greater sense of autonomy and self-determination.

However, being a lone wolf also has drawbacks. One drawback is that individuals who choose this path may miss out on the benefits of social support and connection. They may not have anyone to share their successes or struggles with, which can lead to isolation and loneliness. Additionally, they may not have a support system in place to help them cope with challenges and setbacks.

Another drawback of being a lone wolf is that individuals may not have the opportunity to learn from others or collaborate on projects. They may not have the opportunity to benefit from the knowledge and skills of others, which can limit their growth and development. Additionally, they may not have the opportunity to form meaningful relationships with others, which can be a source of happiness and fulfillment.

The idea of the "lone wolf" or "sigma male" has been glorified in our society, with many people viewing this mentality as a sign of strength and independence. Furthermore, this mindset is often portrayed as the ideal of self-sufficiency and self-reliance, with the belief that one should be able to handle everything on their own without needing the help of others.

However, this glorification of the "lone wolf" mentality can be problematic, particularly when it comes to managing anxiety. Anxiety is a common mental health condition that affects millions of people worldwide, and feelings of worry, fear, and uncertainty characterize it. Individuals who are struggling with anxiety may find it difficult to cope with these feelings on their own, and they may need the support and guidance of others.

Individuals who adopt the "lone wolf" mindset may view seeking help as a sign of weakness or an admission that they are not capable of handling their problems on their own. This can lead to a lack of understanding about the importance of social support in managing anxiety. This is especially concerning since anxiety is a common mental health condition, and many people are affected by it.

Furthermore, the glorification of the "lone wolf" mentality can contribute to the stigmatization of mental health conditions such as anxiety. Many individuals struggling with anxiety may feel ashamed or embarrassed to seek help, and they may be hesitant to reach out to others for fear of being judged. This can lead to a delay in seeking treatment, which can exacerbate anxiety symptoms and lead to more serious mental health issues.

In conclusion, while self-reliance and independence are admirable traits, it's important to consider the importance of social support and connection in managing anxiety. Glorifying the "lone wolf" mentality can be detrimental to one's mental health, as it can lead to a disregard for the importance of social support and contribute to the stigmatization of mental health conditions such as anxiety. Individuals need to understand that seeking help is not a sign of weakness and that social support can be a powerful tool in managing anxiety. It is important to reach out to friends and family, or even professionals, in order to have a support system in place.

The idea of the "lone wolf" mentality is a fallacy, as social connections and support are essential for survival and well-being, not only for humans but also for many other social mammals. For example, studies have shown that social mammals, such as vampire bats, have evolved complex social networks and behaviors that are essential for their survival.

One example of this is the behavior of regurgitation in vampire bats. Vampire bats feed on the blood of other animals, and they can survive for long periods of time without a meal. However, when a bat fails to find a blood meal, it will often rely on the support of its social network to survive. Bats that are unable to find a meal will often approach their roost mates and beg for a regurgitated blood meal. This behavior is known as reciprocal altruism, an essential part of vampire bat social networks.

This example of reciprocal altruism in vampire bats illustrates how social connections and support are essential for survival and well-being. Vampire bats that can rely on their social network for support are more likely to survive and reproduce than those isolated. This is because social connections provide a safety net that can help individuals to cope with difficult situations and to recover from setbacks.

In the same way, human societies also rely on reciprocal altruism, social connections, and support as an essential part of our well-being. While self-reliance and independence are admirable traits, it's important to consider the importance of social support and connection in managing anxiety and other mental health issues. The "lone wolf" mentality is a fallacy, as social connections and support are essential for survival and well-being. Individuals need to understand that seeking help is not a sign of weakness and that social support can be a powerful tool in managing anxiety and other mental health issues.

The idea that the most robust and successful individuals in a community of social mammals seek a "lone wolf" path in life is a misconception. In reality, the most robust and successful individuals often have the most social connections and reciprocated interactions.

Studies have shown that social mammals, such as primates, wolves, elephants, and dolphins, have evolved complex social networks and behaviors essential for their survival and well-being. These social connections provide a sense of belonging, validation, safety, and security, which can help individuals to cope with difficult situations and to recover from setbacks.

In addition, social connections also provide opportunities for individuals to learn from others and collaborate on projects. For example, primates, such as chimpanzees and bonobos, have been observed to share food, tools, and information. Wolves, elephants, and dolphins have also been observed to engage in cooperative hunting, caregiving, and protecting their young.

Furthermore, social connections also provide opportunities for individuals to form meaningful relationships with others, which can be a source of happiness and fulfillment. Studies have shown that social mammals have high emotional intelligence, such as empathy and altruism, which are essential for their social interactions and well-being.

On the other hand, individuals seeking a "lone wolf" path in life may miss out on the many benefits of social connections. For example, they may not have anyone to share their successes or struggles with, which can lead to isolation and loneliness. They may also lack the sense of safety and security that comes with having people in their lives whom they can rely on. In addition, they may not have the opportunity to learn from others or collaborate on projects, limiting their growth and development.

In conclusion, the most robust and successful individuals in a community of social mammals are not the ones who seek a "lone wolf" path in life but the ones who have the most social connections and have the highest amount of reciprocated interactions. Social connections provide a sense of belonging, validation, safety, and security, as well as opportunities for learning and collaboration, and are essential for survival and well-being in social mammals. Individuals need to understand that social connections and support are essential for survival and well-being and that seeking help and support is not a sign of weakness.

Social mammals, such as primates, wolves, elephants, and dolphins, have evolved to perceive the strength of social connections of other individuals and are more likely to engage in altruistic behavior with those with a history of successful reciprocations. This ability is known as "social network cognition," and it enables social mammals to make strategic decisions about social interactions and resource sharing based on the perceived strength of social connections.

One way that social mammals can perceive the strength of social connections is through "social learning." Social learning is the ability to learn from the experiences and behaviors of others, and it enables social mammals to gain information about the social connections of other individuals. For example, primates have been observed to observe the interactions of others and to use this information to make decisions about social interactions and resource sharing.

Another way that social mammals can perceive the strength of social connections is through "social eavesdropping." Social eavesdropping is the ability to gain information about the social connections of other individuals through observation and eavesdropping on their interactions. For example, elephants have been observed to listen to other elephants' vocalizations and use this information to make decisions about social interactions and resource sharing.

The ability of social mammals to perceive the strength of social connections of other individuals also enables them to engage in altruistic behavior with those with a history of successful reciprocations. This is "reciprocal altruism" and is essential to social mammal behavior. For example, vampire bats have been observed to regurgitate blood to other bats that have failed to find a blood meal, and this behavior is thought to be a form of reciprocal altruism.

In conclusion, social mammals have evolved the ability to perceive the strength of social connections of other individuals. They are more likely to engage in altruistic behavior with those who have a history of successful reciprocations. This ability is known as "social network cognition," and it enables social mammals to make strategic decisions about social interactions and resource sharing based on the perceived strength of social connections. This ability is not only limited to social mammals but can also be seen in human societies. Therefore, it is important to understand that altruistic behavior and reciprocation are essential for the survival and well-being of social mammals and humans alike.

Another point is that many people tend to disregard our connection with animals and the similarity between our brains. However, a deeper understanding of this connection can help us to better understand our behavior and emotions from a biological viewpoint.

One of the key similarities between human and animal brains is the presence of neural circuits responsible for basic emotions such as fear, anger, and pleasure. These circuits are evolutionarily ancient and are present in all mammals, including humans. This means many basic emotional responses, such as fear of danger or pleasure in social interactions, are shared with other animals. This understanding can help us to better understand our emotional responses and to see them as a natural part of being a social mammal.

Another similarity between human and animal brains is the presence of neural circuits responsible for social cognition and behavior. These circuits are responsible for our ability to recognize faces, understand social cues, and form social bonds. These circuits are also present in other mammals, such as primates and elephants, and they are thought to be crucial for the survival and well-being of social animals. This understanding can help us to better understand our social behaviors and to see them as a natural part of being a social mammal.

Moreover, studies in neuroscience have also revealed that many of the cognitive processes that we thought were unique to humans, such as language, are not as unique as we thought. For instance, studies of non-human primates, dolphins, and birds have shown that these animals also have the capacity for complex communication and language-like abilities. This understanding can help us to better understand the evolution of human language and to see it as a natural part of being

6.2. Tips for building and maintaining healthy relationships

Building and maintaining healthy relationships is a complex process that involves many different factors. Here are some general tips to help you build and maintain healthy relationships:

6.2.1. Communicate effectively

Open and honest communication is essential for building and maintaining healthy relationships. It is crucial to be able to express your thoughts, feelings and needs clearly and respectfully and to be able to actively listen to the thoughts, feelings, and needs of others.

Effective communication is an essential part of building and maintaining healthy relationships. Here are some tips on how to communicate effectively:

1. Listen actively: Active listening means paying full attention to what the other person is saying and trying to understand their perspective. This means not only hearing the words but also paying attention to nonverbal cues such as body language and tone of voice.

2. Speak clearly and directly: Be clear and direct when expressing your thoughts, feelings, and needs. Avoid using vague or ambiguous language, and avoid being passive-aggressive.

3. Use "I" statements: Use "I" statements to express your thoughts, feelings, and needs. For example, instead of saying, "You're wrong," say, "I disagree." This helps to avoid placing blame or making the other person defensive.

4. Avoid making assumptions: Avoid making assumptions about what the other person is thinking

or feeling. Instead, ask questions and try to understand their perspective.

5. Take a break if needed: If a conversation is becoming heated or emotional, it may be helpful to return to the conversation later. This can help to avoid saying things that you may later regret.

6. Avoid distractions: Avoid distractions such as mobile phones, laptops, or televisions while communicating. This helps the other person to feel heard and respected.

7. Practice empathy: Try to put yourself in the other person's shoes and understand their perspective. Empathy helps to build trust and understanding in a relationship.

8. Be open-minded: Be open-minded to the other person's point of view. Even if you don't agree with them, try to understand where they're coming from.

In conclusion, effective communication is essential to building and maintaining healthy relationships. It involves active listening and clear and direct speaking.

Be empathetic

Empathy is the ability to understand and share the feelings of others. Being compassionate allows you to put yourself in the other person's shoes, which can help you to build trust and understanding in a relationship.

Here are some tips on how to be more empathetic:

1. Practice active listening: Listen carefully to what the other person is saying and try to understand their perspective. Pay attention to their words, body language, and tone of voice.

2. Ask open-ended questions to show that you're interested in understanding the other person's feelings and thoughts.

3. Try to see things from the other person's perspective: Imagine what it would be like to be in their situation and how you would feel in that scenario.

4. Show understanding by acknowledging the other person's feelings, even if you disagree with their perspective.

5. Take time to reflect: Reflect on your emotions and reactions to situations and understand how you would feel in the other person's situation.

6. Practice empathy: Practice empathy in everyday interactions. Try to see things from the other person's perspective and respond with understanding and compassion.

7. Read and educate: Read books and articles, and watch videos about different cultures, perspectives, and life experiences. This will help you to broaden your understanding and empathy for others.

8. Be open to feedback: Be open to feedback and be willing to learn from others. This will help you to become more empathetic and understanding.

Being empathetic is the ability to understand and share the feelings of others. Empathy can be improved through practice, reflection, and education. Empathy is an essential skill that can improve relationships and make you more compassionate and understanding.

Showing appreciation

Showing appreciation is fundamental to strengthening relationships and establishing others are valued. Here are some tips on how to show appreciation:

1. Express verbal gratitude: Say thank you and express your appreciation when someone does something for you.

2. Write a note or letter: A handwritten note or letter can be a meaningful way to express appreciation, especially when expressing appreciation for a significant effort or accomplishment.

3. Show appreciation in public: Publicly recognizing someone's efforts or accomplishments can be a powerful way to show gratitude and inspire others.

4. Give a small gift: A small gift can be a thoughtful way to show appreciation, especially when it is something the person will use or enjoy.

5. Show appreciation through actions: Showing appreciation through activities, such as cooking a meal, doing a chore, or buying a coffee, 's a tangible way of expressing your gratitude.

6. Show appreciation by being present: Showing appreciation by being present and fully engaged in a conversation or activity is a powerful way of expressing gratitude.

7. Show appreciation by being dependable: Showing appreciation by being reliable and following through on commitments is a way of expressing gratitude through actions.

8. Show appreciation by being consistent: Showing appreciation consistently, not only when things are going well but also during difficult times, is a way of expressing gratitude that is more meaningful and genuine.

Showing appreciation is a fundamental way to strengthen relationships, and it's essential to show others that they are valued. Showing appreciation can be achieved through verbal expression, a written message, public recognition, small gifts, actions, dependability, and consistency. It's important to remember that showing appreciation is not a one-time event. It should be a consistent behavior in your relationships.

1. Be flexible: Be willing to compromise, negotiate and be open to change. Be willing to adapt to the changing needs of the relationship.
2. Being willing to compromise, negotiate, and be open to change is essential to building and maintaining healthy relationships. Here are some tips on how to do so:
3. Be open-minded: Be open to new ideas and perspectives, and be willing to consider different options and solutions.
4. Be willing to compromise: Be ready to give and take in a relationship. For example, if your partner wants to go out for dinner but you want to

stay in and cook, consider finding a compromise, such as going out for lunch or cooking together.

5. Be willing to negotiate: Discuss and find a middle ground when there are different opinions or needs. For example, if you and your partner disagree on how to spend your weekends, consider discussing and finding a compromise, such as dedicating one weekend to your preferred activity and the other to your partner's.

6. Be open to change: Be open to change, and be willing to adapt to new situations and challenges. For example, if you and your partner are moving in together and are used to living alone, be open to changing your living habits to accommodate your partner's needs.

7. Practice active listening: Listen to the other person's point of view and try to understand their perspective.

8. Show understanding and willingness to find a solution: Show understanding and willingness to find a solution that works for both parties.

9. Be willing to admit when you're wrong: Be willing to admit when you're wrong and apologize when necessary.

10. Be willing to forgive: Forgive and let go of grudges and resentments.

11. In conclusion, being willing to compromise, negotiate, and be open to change is essential to building and maintaining healthy relationships. It involves being open-minded, willing to

12. Set boundaries: It is important to set healthy boundaries in a relationship, know what you are comfortable with, and communicate this to others. This will help to maintain respect and balance in a relationship.

Setting boundaries

An important aspect of maintaining healthy relationships. Here are some tips on how to set boundaries:

1. Understand your own needs and values: It's important to understand what you're comfortable with and your non-negotiables. For example, if you value alone time, it's important to set boundaries around how much time you spend with others.

2. Communicate your boundaries: Communicate your boundaries to others. For example, if you have difficulty saying "no," practice saying it in a firm but respectful way.

3. Be consistent: Once you've set a boundary, it's important to stick to it. Consistency conveys to others that your boundaries are important to you.

4. Be prepared to enforce your boundaries: Be prepared to take action if your boundaries are crossed. For example, if a friend continually cancels plans at the last minute, you might consider setting a boundary around how much notice they need to give.

5. Be willing to compromise: Be willing to compromise and negotiate on some boundaries and be firm on the non-negotiable ones.

6. Respect others' boundaries: Show respect for others' boundaries and don't take it personally if they set boundaries you don't agree with.

7. Use "I" statements: Use "I" statements when communicating your boundaries. For example, instead of saying, "you're always interrupting me," say, "I feel disrespected when I'm interrupted."

8. Be mindful of your digital boundaries: With the rise of social media, it's important to set boundaries around how you use it and whom you interact with online.

Setting boundaries is an essential aspect of maintaining healthy relationships. It's important to understand your own needs and values, communicate your boundaries, be consistent, be prepared to enforce them, and be willing to compromise and respect others' boundaries. It's also important to set boundaries in the digital world as well.

Take responsibility

To take responsibility for your actions and feelings. Don't blame others for your problems, and take responsibility for your happiness.

1. Taking responsibility for your actions and feelings is important for personal growth and healthy relationships. Here are some tips on how to take responsibility:

2. Recognize your role in a situation: Take the time to reflect on your actions and feelings and how they may have contributed to a situation. For example, consider how your words or actions may have played a role in the conflict if you fought with a friend.

3. Apologize when necessary: Take responsibility for your actions and apologize when necessary. For example, if you said something hurtful to a loved one, take responsibility for your words and apologize for the pain you caused.

4. Learn from your mistakes: Take responsibility for your actions and learn from your mistakes. For example, if you make a mistake at work, take

responsibility for it and work on a plan to prevent it from happening again.

5. Take ownership of your feelings: Recognize that your feelings are valid and important, but also take responsibility for healthily managing them. For example, if you're feeling stressed, take responsibility for finding healthy coping methods, such as exercise or journaling.

6. Don't blame others: Avoid blaming others for your problems or feelings. For example, instead of saying, "You made me feel this way," take responsibility for your feelings and say, "I feel this way."

7. Don't play the victim: Avoid playing the role of a victim and take on a passive attitude. Instead, recognize that you have control over your actions and choices.

8. Don't make excuses: Avoid making excuses for your actions, take responsibility, and find solutions.

9. Lead by example: Lead by example and take responsibility for your actions. It will help others to do the same.

Taking responsibility for your actions and feelings is important for personal growth and healthy relationships. It means recognizing your role in a situation, apologizing when necessary, learning from your mistakes, taking ownership of your feelings, avoiding blame, not playing the victim, not making excuses, and leading by example. It's a continuous process of self-awareness, self-reflection, and self-improvement.

6.2.2. "Triggered"

Being "triggered" refers to the emotional response that occurs when an individual is exposed to a specific stimulus that reminds them of a traumatic event or experience. This emotional response can be intense and overwhelming and lead to various negative behaviors and attitudes. Here I will explore how being "triggered" can be counterproductive and lead to blame and playing the victim.

One of the main problems with being "triggered" is that it can lead to a state of hyperarousal, where an individual's emotional and physiological responses are heightened, making it difficult to think rationally or respond appropriately. This can lead to behavior that is not only counterproductive but also harmful to themselves and others, such as verbal or physical outbursts.

Being "triggered" can also lead to a tendency to blame others for our emotional response. When we are in a state of heightened emotional arousal, taking responsibility for our feelings and actions can be difficult. Instead, we may look for someone else to blame for our emotional response. This can lead to a tendency to play the victim and see ourselves as unfairly treated or targeted by others.

Furthermore, being "triggered" can also lead to a tendency to avoid and suppress the feelings causing the emotional response. This is counterproductive because it prevents us from dealing with the underlying issues and can build up unresolved emotions that can eventually surface negatively.

Being "triggered" can also lead to a tendency to blame society and try to rearrange it according to our belief system. When we are in a state of heightened emotional arousal, it can be easy to see society as the root cause of our problems and to believe that if society were different, we would not be feeling this way. This can lead to a desire to change society to conform to our beliefs and values rather than working to understand and accept the perspectives of others.

For example, an individual who has been the victim of a hate crime may be triggered by the sight of a symbol or flag associated with the perpetrator's group. They may need to advocate for banning that symbol or flag in public spaces, believing it will prevent further hate crimes. However, this approach can be harmful as it can lead to censorship and the suppression of free speech, and it may not address the underlying issue of hate and prejudice in society.

It's important to acknowledge that society is a complex system and changing it is not a simple task. It requires a collective effort from different people with different perspectives and beliefs. It's important to understand that change is a process, and it's not always easy or fast. It's also important to understand that change is not always about making things better for ourselves but rather about creating a better society for everyone.

In conclusion, being "triggered" can lead to a tendency to blame society and try to rearrange it according to our belief system. This approach can be counterproductive and can lead to harmful and divisive actions. It's important to understand that change is a process that requires collaboration, understanding, and patience. It's also important to recognize that society is a complex system and that changing it requires a collective effort from people with different perspectives and beliefs.

While it is true that being "triggered" can lead to a tendency to blame society and try to rearrange it according to our belief system, it is important to acknowledge that change is necessary and that well-informed, self-reflected, integrated, and competent individuals with a healthy moral compass are required to make changes in our system.

Society is not a static entity, and change is a constant process. We must be willing to critically examine our beliefs and values and question whether they align with creating a more just and equitable society. It is important to recognize that change is not always easy and that progress can be slow and incremental. However, change is necessary to create a better future for ourselves and future generations.

To be effective agents of change, we must educate ourselves, seek out diverse perspectives, and engage in open-minded and respectful dialogue with others. We must also be willing to take responsibility for our actions and feelings and to work towards understanding and to accept the perspectives of others.

Moreover, a healthy moral compass is crucial to change-making. It means being guided by values and principles that prioritize the well-being and rights of all members of society, not just a select few. It also means being willing to listen to marginalized and oppressed groups' voices and actively work towards creating a more just and equitable society.

In conclusion, while it is important to recognize that being "triggered" can lead to a tendency to blame society and try to rearrange it according to our belief system, it is equally important to acknowledge that change is necessary. To be effective agents of change, we must be self-reflected, integrated, competent individuals with a healthy moral compass, willing to educate ourselves, seek out diverse perspectives, and engage in open-minded and respectful dialogue with others.

Show interest

Show interest in the lives and interests of others. Take the time to ask questions and be genuinely interested in the other person.

Showing interest in the lives and interests of others is an essential aspect of building and maintaining healthy relationships. Here are some tips on how to do so:

1. Ask open-ended questions that allow the other person to share more about themselves, their interests, and their experiences.

2. Listen actively: Listen attentively and show that you are engaged and interested in what they say.

3. Remember important details: Remember essential details about the other person, such as their hobbies, interests, and milestones. It will show that you care and value the relationship.

4. Show genuine interest: You are genuinely interested in the other person and their life. Ask follow-up questions, show empathy and actively participate in their life.

5. Share your interests: Share your interests and experiences with the other person, and encourage them to share their interests with you.

6. Show interest in their future: Show interest in the other person's future goals and aspirations. For example, ask about their career aspirations and plans and how you can support them in achieving them.

7. Make time for them: Make time for the other person, and show that you value spending time with them.

8. Show interest in their family and friends: Show interest in the other person's family and friends, and try to get to know them.

9. In conclusion, showing interest in the lives and interests of others is an important aspect of building and maintaining healthy relationships. It involves asking open-ended questions, listening actively, remembering important details, showing genuine interest, sharing your interests, showing interest in their future, and making time for them and their family and friends. It's important to remember that building a relationship is a two-way street, and showing interest in others will allow them to show interest in you.

Practice forgiveness

Forgiveness is important in building and maintaining healthy relationships. Holding onto grudges and resentments can poison a relationship.

Forgiveness is letting go of resentment, anger, and negative feelings toward someone who has wronged us. It is an essential aspect of maintaining healthy relationships and personal well-being. Here are some tips on how to practice forgiveness:

1. Recognize the hurt: Acknowledge and accept the hurt you have experienced due to the other person's actions. It's essential to validate your feelings and understand that being hurt is a normal response to being wronged.

2. Let go of anger: Understand that anger and resentment will only keep you from moving forward. Instead, practice mindfulness, talk to a therapist or a friend, and find healthy ways to release the anger.

3. Find empathy: Try understanding the other person's perspective and reasons for their actions. Of course, this doesn't excuse their behavior, but it can help to see the situation from a different angle.

4. Decide to forgive: Make a conscious decision to forgive the other person. This doesn't mean that you

have to forget what happened or that you have to continue a relationship with them, but it means letting go of the negative feelings toward them.

5. Practice forgiveness regularly: Forgiveness is not a one-time event but requires continuous practice. It's important to remind yourself of your decision to forgive and let go of negative feelings.

6. Don't expect apologies: Forgiving someone doesn't mean they will apologize for their behavior. Some people may not even recognize that they have wronged you. Forgiving is about letting go of resentment, not about receiving apologies.

7. Seek professional help: If you find it hard to forgive, seek professional help. A therapist can help you to understand your feelings and to find ways to forgive.

Forgiveness is not always easy, and it doesn't mean that you have to forget what happened or that you have to continue a relationship with the person. But it is a crucial step to move on from resentment and negative feelings and to find inner peace.

Building and maintaining healthy relationships require effort and time, but it's worth it. The key is to communicate effectively and be empathetic.

6.3. How to find and participate in support groups

Support groups are a powerful tool for coping with a common issue or challenge. They provide a safe and supportive environment where individuals can share their experiences, feelings, and insights with others who understand and relate to their situation. In addition, support groups can benefit people with various issues, including mental health conditions, chronic illnesses, and life transitions.

To find a support group, there are several options. One way to find support groups is to check with local hospitals, clinics, or community centers. Many of these organizations offer support groups for individuals with specific conditions or challenges. Additionally, many national organizations and advocacy groups for specific requirements offer support groups for individuals living with that condition.

Another way to find support groups is to search online. Many online support groups can be accessed through various websites or social media platforms. These groups can be a great option for individuals who live in rural areas or who may have mobility or transportation issues.

Knowing the type of support group you are looking for is also important. For example, some groups are led by professionals while others are peer-led, some groups are open, and others are closed. Open groups are generally open to new members, and closed groups are typically reserved for a specific group of individuals.

When participating in a support group, it's important to be respectful of others and to follow the group's guidelines and rules. It's also important to be mindful of your emotional state and to take care of yourself if the discussion becomes too emotional.

It's essential to remember that support groups aren't a substitute for professional therapy but can be a valuable supplement to an individual's treatment plan. In addition, they can provide emotional support, validation, and a sense of community, which can be incredibly valuable for individuals coping with a difficult situation.

7. Conclusion: Moving Forward

7.1. Summary

Here is a summary of the key concepts covered in the book.

7.1.1. What is anxiety?

Anxiety is a normal emotional response to stress and uncertainty. Feelings of worry, nervousness, and unease characterize it. Anxiety can manifest in different ways, such as physical symptoms (e.g., increased heart rate, sweating, muscle tension) and cognitive symptoms (e.g., worry, rumination, and obsessive thoughts). Anxiety can be a normal response to stressors and can be beneficial in small doses. Still, it can be diagnosed as an anxiety disorder when it becomes excessive, persistent, and interferes with daily life. Anxiety disorders are the world's most common mental health conditions, including Generalized Anxiety Disorder, Panic Disorder, Social Anxiety Disorder, Specific Phobia, and others. They can be treated with therapy, medication, or a combination.

7.1.2. What role does biology play in anxiety?

Hormones and neurotransmitters play an important role in regulating anxiety in men. Hormones such as cortisol, released in response to stress, can affect the body's "fight or flight" response, leading to physical symptoms of anxiety such as increased heart rate and blood pressure.

Neurotransmitters, such as serotonin and GABA, are chemicals that transmit signals in the brain and play a key role in regulating mood and anxiety. For example, low levels of serotonin have been linked to anxiety and depression, while low levels of GABA have been linked to feelings of worry and nervousness.

Testosterone, a primary male sex hormone, also affects anxiety. Research suggests that low testosterone levels can lead to increased anxiety symptoms, while testosterone replacement therapy may reduce anxiety in men.

Additionally, research has suggested that men may have different neural pathways and responses to stress and anxiety than women. For example, men tend to have a more active hypothalamic-pituitary-adrenal (HPA) axis, a system responsible for the body's stress response. This may make them more susceptible to the physical symptoms of anxiety, such as increased heart rate and blood pressure.

In summary, hormones and neurotransmitters play a significant role in regulating anxiety in men. Hormones like cortisol and the primary male sex hormone testosterone, and neurotransmitters like serotonin and GABA, are all linked to anxiety and may influence the way men experience and process anxiety. Additionally, men may have different neural pathways and responses to stress and anxiety than women, making them more susceptible to the physical symptoms of anxiety.

7.1.3. Past events

Exposure to traumatic events, such as physical or emotional abuse, loss of a loved one, or job loss, can have a significant and long-lasting impact on an individual's mental health, including the development of anxiety. In addition, trauma can lead to changes in brain chemistry, which can contribute to the development of anxiety disorders.

7.1.4. Mindfulness and anxiety

Mindfulness is a practice that involves paying attention to the present moment in a non-judgmental way. It can be used as a tool to manage anxiety in men by helping them to focus on the present rather than worrying about the future or dwelling on the past. Mindfulness can be practiced through various techniques such as meditation, yoga, deep breathing exercises, and body scans.

Mindfulness-based interventions are effective in reducing anxiety symptoms in men. In addition, the practice of mindfulness can help men to:

1. Recognize negative thoughts and emotions: Mindfulness can help men to become more aware of their thoughts and feelings, which can help them to recognize negative thoughts and emotions that contribute to anxiety.

2. Accept and cope with difficult emotions: Mindfulness can help men to accept difficult emotions and to develop coping skills to manage them.

3. Decrease rumination: Mindfulness can help men stop ruminating on negative thoughts and emotions, reducing anxiety symptoms.

4. Increase self-awareness: Mindfulness can help men to increase self-awareness, which can help them to

understand their thought patterns and reactions to stress.

5. Increase well-being: Mindfulness can help men improve well-being by reducing stress and anxiety and increasing positive emotions.

Mindfulness and Journaling are two techniques that can be used to battle anxiety. Mindfulness is a practice that involves paying attention to the present moment in a non-judgmental way, and it can be used to increase self-awareness and reduce stress and anxiety. Journaling is a technique that involves writing down thoughts and feelings in a diary or notebook. It can be used to help individuals gain insight into their thoughts and emotions, identify patterns and triggers, and develop coping strategies. These practices can be used together to provide a comprehensive approach to managing anxiety.

7.1.5. Self-Care

Self-care can include a variety of practices, such as exercise, healthy eating, getting enough sleep, and engaging in hobbies and activities that bring enjoyment.

Self-care practices, such as exercise, healthy eating, getting enough sleep, and practicing relaxation techniques, can help reduce anxiety by promoting physical and emotional well-being. Additionally, setting boundaries, engaging in joyful activities, and connecting with others can help alleviate anxiety. However, it is important to note that self-care should be part of a comprehensive treatment plan for anxiety, and individuals should consult with a healthcare professional for personalized advice.

Scheduling can help reduce anxiety by providing a sense of structure and organization, making it easier to manage daily tasks and responsibilities. Individuals can plan their day, prioritize tasks, and set realistic goals by creating a schedule. This can help reduce feelings of overwhelming and uncertainty, which are common triggers for anxiety. Additionally, scheduling time for self-care activities, such as exercise, relaxation techniques, and socializing, can help alleviate anxiety by promoting physical and emotional well-being.

7.1.6. CBT

Cognitive-behavioral therapy (CBT) is a type of psychotherapy focusing on the relationship between thoughts, feelings, and behaviors. This treatment approach is highly effective in treating anxiety disorders.

The benefits of CBT for anxiety include:

1. Helping individuals identify and change negative thought patterns and beliefs that contribute to anxiety
2. Teaching practical coping skills and problem-solving strategies for managing anxiety
3. Providing a sense of control and empowerment over anxiety symptoms
4. Improving communication and relationship skills
5. Giving individuals the tools to maintain progress over time, CBT is considered a "gold standard" treatment for anxiety disorders, and it's often recommended as a first-line treatment by healthcare professionals. It's also relatively short-term, and its effectiveness can be seen in as little as 12 weeks.

7.1.7. Alternative Therapies

Alternative anxiety therapies refer to treatments that are not considered part of conventional Western medicine, such as herbal remedies, acupuncture, mindfulness, and yoga.

While alternative anxiety therapies may offer a range of potential benefits, they may also have potential drawbacks. Therefore, it is important to consult with a healthcare professional to evaluate the appropriateness and safety of alternative therapy in each case. They can help to weigh the risks and benefits and help determine if an alternative therapy is an appropriate course of action for treating an individual's anxiety.

7.1.8. Supplements

In conclusion, omega-3 fatty acids, magnesium, L-Theanine, valerian root, passionflower, kava, and ashwagandha are all-natural remedies and supplements that have been shown to help reduce symptoms of anxiety.

It's worth noting that these remedies may not be appropriate for everyone and should be used in conjunction with traditional therapies. Additionally, it's important to consult with a healthcare professional before taking any supplements or natural remedies, as they may interact with any medications you take or have any adverse effects. Finally, it's also important to ensure the products are sourced from reputable manufacturers to guarantee the purity and quality of the product.

7.1.9. Social Support

Social support and connection are crucial factors in managing anxiety. Studies have shown that individuals with strong social support networks have lower levels of anxiety and depression compared to those who lack social connections. This is because social support can provide a sense of belonging and validation, which can help to counteract feelings of isolation and self-doubt.

The idea that the most robust and successful individuals in a community of social mammals seek a "lone wolf" path in life is a misconception. In reality, the most robust and successful individuals often have the most social connections and reciprocated interactions.

Creating healthy social connections can involve several steps:

1. First, identify your interests and values: Identifying what you are passionate about and what is important to you can help you find people with similar interests and values.
2. Seek opportunities to connect: Find opportunities to connect with others through social events, clubs, groups, or organizations that align with your interests and values.
3. Be open and approachable: Be open to meeting new people and be approachable when interacting with others. Smile, make eye contact, and actively listen when engaging in conversation.
4. Be authentic: Be true to yourself, and don't be afraid to share your thoughts, feelings, and experiences with others.

5. Invest in existing relationships: Nurture and maintain relationships by reaching out, spending time together, and showing appreciation.

6. Be persistent: Building healthy social connections take time and effort, so be persistent in your efforts and don't give up if you don't make a connection immediately.

It's important to remember that creating healthy social connections is a process, and finding the right people who align with your interests and values may take time. But by being open, approachable, and persistent, you can gradually build a supportive network of people to help you navigate life's challenges, including anxiety.

7.2. To conclude

Battling anxiety is a long-term project that requires discipline on several fronts. First, it involves a commitment to taking care of your physical and emotional well-being and making lifestyle changes that can help reduce anxiety symptoms. This may include regular exercise, healthy eating, getting enough sleep, practicing relaxation techniques, and engaging in enjoyable activities. Additionally, it may involve seeking professional help, such as therapy or medication, and learning coping strategies to manage anxiety effectively.

It is important to take your mental health seriously and to understand that anxiety is a real and treatable condition. While it may take time and effort to manage, by making a commitment to your mental health and following through with a comprehensive treatment plan, you can experience significant improvements in your overall well-being. Remember, you are not alone in this journey; many resources are available to help you cope with and overcome anxiety.

Encouragement to continue practicing the strategies learned.

Remember that anxiety is a normal part of life, and it's important to continue using the techniques and approaches you've learned. These tools have helped you in the past and will continue to be effective if you keep using them. It can be easy to fall back into old patterns, but try to remind yourself that you have the power to manage your anxiety. Stay consistent with your practice, and you'll see improvement over time.

It's also important to remind yourself that setbacks are a normal part of the process. It's okay if you have a bad day or things don't go as planned. It doesn't mean that you're not making progress or that you're not capable of managing your anxiety. Just keep pushing forward, and don't give up. You've come this far, and you're making progress. Keep going and trust in yourself and your abilities. Remember that it's not a failure to seek help if you need it; it's a sign of strength. You got this.

And most importantly, be kind and compassionate to yourself. Remember that you are doing the best you can and not alone in your struggles with anxiety. You are not defined by your anxiety and are more than capable of overcoming it. Give yourself credit for taking steps to manage your anxiety and remind yourself that you are capable of change. Remember to take care of yourself, and don't hesitate to reach out to loved ones, friends, or professionals for support. You are strong, and you can do this.

Information on where to find additional resources for managing anxiety

There are a variety of resources available for men who want to manage their anxiety, such as podcasts and books.

Podcasts:

"The Anxiety Guy" by Scott Symington offers practical tips and strategies for managing anxiety.

"The Anxiety Coaches Podcast" by Gina Ryan and Alec Miller provides information and support for individuals with anxiety.

"Anxiety Slayer" by Shann Vander Leek focuses on mindfulness and self-compassion as tools for managing anxiety.

"The Jordan Peterson Podcast" by Jordan B. Peterson, a famous clinical psychologist and bestselling author, touches upon anxiety and meaning in his podcasts and books.

"The Huberman Lab Podcast" by Dr. Andrew Huberman, a professor at Stanford University, indulges in in-depth conversations about self-optimization and neurobiology.

Books:

"The Anxiety Toolkit" by Alice Boyes provides practical strategies for managing anxiety.

"The Mindfulness and Acceptance Workbook for Anxiety" by John P. Forsyth and Georg H. Eifert focuses on using mindfulness and acceptance-based techniques to manage anxiety.

"Feeling Good: The New Mood Therapy" by David D. Burns offers cognitive-behavioral techniques for managing depression and anxiety.

"Man's Search for Meaning" by Viktor Frankl is a classic book that explores the human experience of suffering, particularly in the context of the Holocaust, and how to find meaning and purpose in life, which can help to reduce anxiety.

My heartfelt thanks.

I appreciate that you bought my book. It means a lot to me. The competition was intense, but you still chose me.

So, I wanted to say a heartfelt thank you.

However, if you have a spare second, would you consider leaving me a review on amazon? It is the easiest way to support me. The struggle is real.

It would mean a lot to me!

>> Leave a review on Amazon US <<

>> Leave a review on Amazon UK <<

Printed in Great Britain
by Amazon

24334329R00101